AVID

READER

PRESS

We Need to Hang Out

A Memoir of Making Friends

Billy Baker

Avid Reader Press

New York   London   Toronto   Sydney   New Delhi

Avid Reader Press
An Imprint of Simon & Schuster, Inc.
1230 Avenue of the Americas
New York, NY 10020

First Avid Reader Press hardcover edition January 2021

AVID READER PRESS and colophon are trademarks of Simon & Schuster, Inc.

For information about special discounts for bulk purchases,
please contact Simon & Schuster Special Sales
at 1-866-506-1949 or business@simonandschuster.com.

The Simon & Schuster Speakers Bureau can bring authors to your live event.
For more information or to book an event, contact the
Simon & Schuster Speakers Bureau at 1-866-248-3049
or visit our website at www.simonspeakers.com.

Interior design by Ruth Lee-Mui

Portions of this book appeared, in different form, in the *Boston Globe*.

Manufactured in the United States of America

1   3   5   7   9   10   8   6   4   2

Library of Congress Cataloging-in-Publication Data has been applied for.

ISBN 978-1-9821-1108-3
ISBN 978-1-9821-1111-3 (ebook)

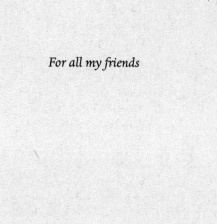

For all my friends

Author's Note

The story in this book was concluding just as COVID-19 appeared. In forcing us apart, it reminded us why we are better together.

We Need to Hang Out

One

*L*et's start with the moment I realized I was already a loser, which was just after I was more or less told that I was destined to become one.

I had been summoned to a magazine editor's office with one of the oldest lies in journalism: "We have a story we think you'd be perfect for." This is how editors talk when they're about to try to con you into doing something you won't want to do. The lie remains in circulation because it works well on the right sort of ego.

Which is precisely how yours truly found himself rising from his desk in the City Room of the old *Boston Globe* building to make the winding walk to the other end of the compound, back to where they kept the people who made the Sunday magazine. I knocked at the door of the offending editor, plopped down in a chair across from his desk, and told him to lay it on me.

"We want you to write about how middle-aged men have no friends," he said.

Excuse me, pal?

He didn't wait for a response, and moved quickly through his argument, flipping through papers on his desk and windows on his computer as he laid out the evidence for his thesis: There was a crisis in modern friendship, and it was having a catastrophic effect on mental and physical health.

I have plenty of friends, buddy. Are you calling me a loser? You are.

Also, did you just call me middle-aged?

He paid no attention to the fact that my face was clearly torn between wanting to fight and wanting to cry and arrived at his big finale, one of the most time-tested lies in all of journalism.

"You'll have fun with it!" he said.

Finally, silence signaled that it was my turn to talk, but I had no good answer to his pitch. I was only just beginning to process the question.

"I'll think about it," I told the editor. This is how reporters talk when they're trying to get out of something they don't want to do.

As I slunk back to my desk, I ran a quick mental roll call just to confirm that I was not, in fact, perfect for this story of loneliness.

First off, there was my buddy Mark. We went to high school together, and we still talked all the time, and we hung out all the . . .

Wait, how often did we actually hang out? Maybe four or five times a year? Maybe less?

Then there was my other best friend from high school, Rory . . .

I genuinely could not remember the last time I'd seen Rory. Had it been a year? Entirely possible.

Then there was my brother, Jack, but he had moved to California after college and we were lucky if we saw each other twice a year.

I continued down the mental list, racing through my good friends, my great friends, my lifelong friends, the people who sure as shit better show up at my funeral. Most of them felt like they were still in my life, but why? Because I knew what their kids looked like from Facebook? It had been years since I'd last seen most of them. Decades for a few. How can days feel so long but years feel so short?

By the time I made it back to my desk chair, the waves of disappointment were already washing over me, and I knew that anger would be close behind.

That editor was right. I was indeed perfect for this story. Not because I was unusual in any way, but because I was painfully typical.

And if that stupid editor had his facts straight, it meant I was heading down a dangerous path.

I'd turned forty the previous year. I had a wife and two young boys, and we had recently purchased a fairly ugly home with aluminum siding in a small coastal town about an hour north of the city. In our driveway were two aging station wagons with crushed Goldfish crackers serving as floor mats. When I stepped on a Lego in the middle of the night on the way to the bathroom, I told myself it was cute that I'd turned into a sitcom dad.

During the week, much of my waking life revolved around

work. Or getting ready for work. Or driving to work. Or driving home from work. Or texting my wife to tell her I was going to be late getting home from work.

Yes, I had friends at work, but those were accidents of proximity. I rarely saw those people anywhere outside of the office.

Most of everything else revolved around my children. I spent a lot of time asking them where their shoes were, and they spent a lot of time asking me when they could have some "Dada time." Each time I heard that phrase, it melted my heart and paralyzed me with guilt, for they tended to ask for it in moments when they sensed I couldn't give it to them—when I was distracted by an email on my phone, or holed up in the spare bedroom hammering out a story on deadline, or dealing with the constant, boring logistics of running a home.

We could usually squeeze in an hour of "Dada time" before bed—mostly wrestling or reading books—and I was pretty good about squeezing in an hour of "me time" each day, which usually meant getting up before dawn to go to the gym or for a run before it was time to begin looking for my kids' shoes.

But when you added everything up, there was no real "friend time" left. Without even realizing it, I had structured myself into being a loser.

"You should use this story as a call to do something about it."

That's Richard Schwartz. He's a psychiatrist, and I had called him because my editor told me to call him. I'm a first-ballot hall-of-famer when it comes to avoiding unflattering reflections, so talking to a shrink was not at the top of the list of things I wanted to do at the moment. But Schwartz was a local Boston guy who had written a book with his wife, Dr. Jacqueline Olds, called *The Lonely American: Drifting Apart in the Twenty-First Century*, which I found shelved in the "Body & Soul" section at the library. Reluctantly, I rang him up.

Schwartz seemed like a good dude, and he quickly came to two easy conclusions about me: My story was very typical, and my story was very dangerous.

When people become over-scheduled, he told me, they don't shortchange their kids or their careers. No, they shortchange their friendships. "And the public health dangers of that are incredibly clear," Schwartz said with appropriate gravitas.

Beginning in the 1980s, study after study started to show that people who were socially isolated from their friends—regardless of how healthy their family lives were—proved far more susceptible to a massive list of health problems, and were far more likely to die during a given period than their socially connected peers. And this was after correcting for things like age and gender and lifestyle choices.

Loneliness kills. And in the twenty-first century, by any reasonable measure, loneliness has become an epidemic.

"Loneliness" is a subjective state, where the distress you feel comes from the discrepancy between the social connections you desire and the social connections you actually have. That's not a very high bar. That sounds a lot like me. That sounds a lot like everyone.

You can feel lonely when you are alone. But you can also feel lonely in a crowd. However loneliness arrives, its consequences are terrible. Name a health condition you don't want and there's a study linking it to loneliness. Diabetes. Obesity. Alzheimer's. Heart disease. Cancer. One study found that in terms of damage to your health, loneliness was the equivalent of smoking 15 cigarettes a day.

Now consider that a 2019 survey found that 61 percent of Americans are measurably lonely, based on how they scored on the UCLA Loneliness Scale, the gold standard for decades. That percentage had jumped seven points from just the previous year. And according to a large study conducted by the AARP, more than 42 million Americans over the age of 45 suffer from "chronic loneliness."

It gets worse. A massive study by Brigham Young University, using data from 3.5 million people collected over 35 years, found that individuals who suffered from loneliness, isolation, or even those who simply lived alone saw their risk of premature death rise by up to 32 percent.

More people live alone today than at any point in human history. In the United States, 27 percent of households are single-person. In 1970, that number was 17 percent. For older Americans, those numbers are even higher. Nearly a third of people above the age of 65 live alone. By age 86, the percentage has jumped to half.

While loneliness clearly poses a gigantic issue in our society, Schwartz told me, dealing with it is extremely difficult for one simple reason: No one wants to admit that they're lonely.

"Since my wife and I have written about loneliness and social isolation, we see a fair number of people for whom this is a big problem," Schwartz said. "But very often, they don't come in saying they're lonely. Most people have the experience you had in your editor's office—admitting you're lonely feels very much like admitting you're a loser. Psychiatry has worked hard to destigmatize things like depression, and to a large part it has been successful. People are comfortable saying they're depressed. But they're not comfortable saying they're lonely, because you're the kid sitting alone in the cafeteria."

I've never been that kid. I'm gregarious and outgoing. I've never had trouble making friends. I'm fairly good about keeping in touch. Or at least I comment on their Facebook posts, and they comment on mine.

My wife and I got together with other couples every now and again. And I'd even gone on a few "guy dates" with newer acquaintances I'd met through my kids or on an assignment or wherever. But all too often those seemed to be one and done. We'd go grab a couple beers, and then spend those beers talking about how we're over-scheduled and never get to do things like this, while vaguely making plans to do something again, though we both know it will probably never happen. It's a polite way of kicking the ball down the road but never into the goal. I like you. You like me. Is that enough? Is this what passes for friendship at this stage in life?

Schwartz had convinced me of many things in our conversation, but he had failed to get me to admit that I was lonely. Nope, not me. I was simply a textbook case of the silent majority of people who won't admit they're starved for friendship, even if all signs point to the contrary.

• • •

Before he let me off the phone, Schwartz again urged me to take this as a call to action. He suggested finding activities with built-in regularity, and I didn't need a PhD to understand why that's the favored advice of the experts who work in this field. As the doctors would say, planning anything suuuucks. Scheduling takes initiative, and if you have to take initiative every time you see a friend, it's easy for the effort to feel like yet another aggravation you don't need. Anyone who has ever been on an email chain trying to plan a group get-together knows how quickly the aggravation can kill the concept. Too often, the moment of joy doesn't come from actually seeing your friends; it comes from the aggravation ending.

So the expert recommendation is rather grandfatherly—join a bowling league. Essentially.

The other advice is to pick up the phone, which is a problem if you're like me, which is to say a guy. I hate talking on the phone. This is a very typical male objection, and it's a known barrier to friendship. For women, however, the phone is a tool for strengthening friendship. Not long after I hung up with Schwartz, I read an article about a recent talk given by an Oxford professor named Robin Dunbar, who presented a study showing that women—but not men—can maintain close relationships over the phone. My wife is capable of having long phone conversations with her sister and her friends, and I stare in amazement as she paces about in the kitchen. Every phone conversation I have with one of my buddies seems to last about 45 seconds before one of us says "All right, I'll catch up with you later."

Men need an activity to bond. This finding is supported in study after study, or from pulling your head out of your ass and simply looking around. It's a measurable fact that men make their deepest friendships through periods of intense engagement, such as sports or military service or school. It's hardwired into our genetics; we spent millions of years hunting together. Going through something together was not only how we built our bonds but how we maintained them.

Here's a tidbit that'll have you staring off into the distance and nodding your head (at least that's what I did when Schwartz told me about it during our first conversation). So apparently psychologists and sociologists do studies where they creep around and take photos of people unawares, and then analyze them for patterns. And when they look at snapshots of people interacting, an unmistakable distinction emerges between how men and women orient themselves to one another and the world.

Women talk face-to-face. Men talk shoulder to shoulder.

Once this was pulled into focus for me, I couldn't not see it. The evidence is everywhere. Barstools and box seats are designed for it. Even in situations where men are seated across a table from one another, I noticed that they naturally angle their seats away from one another, facing in the same direction, staring out at the world together.

This all had me thinking about a big activity I had recently been through with a friend. I'd run the Boston Marathon with a buddy from college named Matt. He lived outside Chicago, but as we went through our training we were in regular contact about how much we hated running, and those conversations led to other things, and before I had really noticed it we were closer than we'd ever been, even though our longest actual conversation was in the four-ish hours it took us to get from Hopkinton to Boston. We repeated the entire cycle seven months later at the Chicago Marathon, and it was a fantastic thing to go through with a buddy. I never could have done it without him. But since the day we crossed that finish line in Grant Park, I'd had almost zero contact with Matt. We were no longer going through anything together.

I suppose I could call him or something, but I hate the phone.

When I looked around at my life, there was much to be happy about. If I needed a confidant, I was lucky to have married the right woman. My kids were the best. Everyone in my inner circle was healthy and stable. All the pieces were there. Except for my friends. They weren't even on the to-do list. And the saddest part was how normal that had come to feel.

I missed my friends. And I had to believe they missed me. Was I really supposed to wait until we could reunite on the golf course after we'd retired? This stupid assignment had shown me that our isolation was not only sad but quite dangerous. Like, shockingly dangerous. Like a greased slide into a pit filled with spikes.

But I had an idea. Or, more accurately, I was going to steal an idea.

Shortly after we'd moved from the city to Cape Ann, I took a kayaking class run out of a small shop in Essex that led paddling tours through the Great Marsh. The shop was owned by an older guy named Ozzie and his wife, Sandy, and at some point I heard Ozzie decline an invitation because he had Wednesday Night.

I didn't totally follow, as I was under the impression that we all had Wednesday night, but Ozzie explained that "Wednesday Night" was a pact that he and some buddies had made many years before, a standing order that on Wednesday nights they would get together and do something. Anything.

Everything about the idea sounded perfect to me, a blend of quaint and profound, right down to its name, which is a lack of a name, which is a very guy thing to do. Also . . . Wednesdays. Ain't nothing great about Wednesdays.

But above all, what struck me was the fact that he and his buddies had been doing it for decades. There was a hidden sweetness to the gesture, and Ozzie was not a soft guy. No, this was the simple acknowledgment from male friends that they needed their guys for no other reason than they just did.

The moment he explained the concept to me, I knew I was going to steal it. You know, when I was older and needed something like that.

Three years later, as I worked on that stupid article, I realized I had already waited too long.

Two

The deadline is always the ultimate inspiration, so I went through my usual routine of waking up early, pounding coffee until I was peeing like I was pregnant, then staring at my computer screen and panicking.

What the hell was I doing? What was this story about? That I'm a loser? Fine. I admit it.

I typed out my complaints, blamed my editor for the con job, threw in some research, and unapologetically raised my hand and took the L.

The whole thing kind of made me laugh as I typed, if I'm honest. That's probably psychopath behavior. But it had been such a strange trip since I got up from that editor's chair, convinced that I was going to prove him wrong.

Instead, I had been forced to admit that I had no truly active friendships. Just as painfully, I had to admit that I was middle-aged.

Whatever. At least I had completed the stupid assignment. No one was going to read this story anyway. Who the hell wants to talk about "loneliness"? Emily Dickinson called it "the horror not to be surveyed," and she's a woman who lay in bed and wrote poems about death.

A few weeks later, I was seated in front of a microphone in a studio at National Public Radio, already well into my reign as America's #1 Middle-Aged Loser, speaking live to the nation and feeling like something heavy was about to collapse.

Dr. Schwartz was seated to my left, and thus far in the program we'd shared a lively discussion about my article and what a loser I was. Then the host of the program announced that he was going to patch in the Surgeon General of the United States from Washington.

Dr. Vivek Murthy's voice came over my headphones, and straightaway the host challenged him to have my back. "What do you think of this notion that middle-aged men in America let their friendships slide, and it's consequential?"

I hated the word "notion," if only because it perfectly captured the self-doubt that gurgled in the pit of my stomach, the impostor syndrome that had overtaken me since the article had published and unleashed madness into my life. What did I know about public health? I'm not a doctor. I'm just some guy who was trying to wriggle out of an assignment he didn't want. I probably misinterpreted everything. Instead of covering the story, I probably twisted it to fit me.

I feared a huge correction coming on. But instead the good doctor had my back. His response was all affirmation and encouragement, a sweeping validation that the response I was receiving—which we'll get to in a moment—was not an anomaly but instead the great rumbling of a silent, lonely majority. My better suspicions were true: I had not gone too far; instead, I had not gone far enough. Friendship was in crisis. Something fundamental had broken. Something needed to be fixed.

"Well, it rings true, not just for middle-aged men but for populations across the board," Dr. Murthy said in response to the host's query. "One of the things we've come to realize is that loneliness is an underappreciated public health threat. In the 1980s, about twenty percent of adults said that they were lonely. Now that number stands at forty percent, and I believe that's likely an underrepresentation because many people don't report loneliness because they fear the stigma around loneliness. So we're talking here about a subjective state. You can have dozens of friends and acquaintances and still feel lonely."

He rattled off the frightening list of consequences, which I still found hard to believe, and the simple conclusion:

"Loneliness is toxic for your health."

The story, as reluctant as I had been to admit it, was abundantly clear.

We, my friends, were in the midst of a full-blown loneliness epidemic, one that would only become worse with the arrival of a virus that forced us apart.

And by raising my hand and admitting I was a bit of a loser, I found myself standing at the dead center of the gathering storm.

● ● ●

Magazines have a long lag time, so a few weeks passed between when I wrote the original article and when it was published, and I mostly forgot about it. Or, rather, I avoided thinking about the fact that I was about to publicly admit that I had let many of my close friendships slip away as I structured myself into a work-family-work cycle that left me feeling like a loser.

I could no longer deny how well my symptoms fit the diagnosis that had been handed to me. But identifying a problem and knowing how to fix it aren't the same thing, and whenever I did think about trying to fix my friend problems, I felt like I had no clue how to begin. I couldn't just call up guys I hadn't seen in forever and tell them I missed them, right? I needed some sort of in-between, some reason for that to happen.

On a Thursday in early March, I was working from home, sitting at my desk, when I got an email from a reader about the article, which the magazine had apparently just published online, a few days before the print magazine hit the stands.

It was a nice, personal note from a guy in Ohio who said he used to have a "Wednesday Night" with his buddies—in their case, it was "First Tuesday of the Month"—but the tradition had faded as they entered their forties, and now at 53 he was wondering where everyone had gone.

Soon there came another email. And another. And another. Then it just snowballed. In an instant, my inbox was overflowing. I received thousands of emails from people all over the United States, and *tons* of emails from men in Australia and Alberta, of all places. It quickly became one of the most popular articles that the *Boston Globe* had ever published, and as the odometer rolled past a million readers, it felt like every one of them sent me a personal email, to the point that the magazine offered to give me an intern to help handle the flood.

I declined the offer and resolved to reply to each heartfelt message, no matter how long it took, because each came from a person who needed to feel seen.

Many of the emails were perfectly precise. "This is me" or "I feel like you crawled into my brain." Others offered some version of "I sent the article to my buddies and now we're getting the band back together." Those ones always felt great.

But there were hundreds and hundreds of emails that went so much deeper than that, long and emotional. I heard from young people saying they felt like they had a thousand "friends" and none at all. I heard from older people telling me I didn't know the half of it. And I heard from the desperately lonely asking if they could come to my "Wednesday Night."

The response from men in my age demographic—those at the beginning of middle age—was huge, but there was a similarly huge response from those on the tail end of middle age. Some offered tips on what had worked for them. Many others wrote: "I wish I'd read this 20 years ago." My aunt pulled me aside to say she was worried about her husband, who had lost his relationships with all the other "sports dads" on the sideline when his kids had grown. My own mother had a frank talk with my dad about getting out more.

A vast conversation had begun, branching off in ways that I hadn't even considered. The editor who had originally dumped the assignment on me was my age, the father of young kids. We were looking at this issue through a straw; it should have been a fish-eye lens.

I received letters from those who were divorced or widowed telling me how their social circle had disappeared in an instant; from those who had moved to a new place and knew no one; from people who felt truly isolated from the world around them and didn't know how to reconnect. Readers asked lots of questions about things I had not researched, like the impact of social media or the role of loneliness in the addiction epidemic. Many sent me studies I hadn't seen, studies that showed the spokes of this problem extending into all corners of the modern world. Combined together, it built the argument that a species that thrived on its social connections—*the* social animal—was falling apart as we moved away from that core.

I had neglected women in my article, and many of them wrote me to say: "Hey, what about us?" I had focused on men because the data suggested they had it worse, but loneliness was far from a male exclusive. And if I'm honest: I was afraid to write about women, because the only thing I know about women with absolute certainty is that they don't want a man telling them how they feel. But that reasoning was an easy cop-out. For when I thought of the friendships I missed, it was not just my guys but also the many women I considered lifelong friends but had drifted away from for the exact same reasons—everyone was locked into important commitments that didn't include friendship.

Friends were what we did after the "important" stuff was done, and that shit is never done.

According to time-use statistics from the U.S. Department of

Labor, spending time with friends is so far down on the list of how we go about our days that it's amazing we still remember their names. Work is the biggest time-suck. Shocker. Sleep comes a close second, though the two grow ever apart. What's left is about five hours per day in a broad category known as "leisure." This includes exercising and socializing, but the sad fact is that more than half of that time is spent watching television. "The principal contributor to loneliness in this country is television," the anthropologist Ashley Montagu opined many decades ago. "What happens is the family 'gets together' alone." Even in 2017, people between the ages of 15 and 44, the original smartphone junkies, were still logging a solid two hours a day with the boob tube. Older people watch much more. Socializing and communicating—which includes everything from calling a friend to hosting a party to chatting at the watercooler—occupy an average of just 39 minutes per day. Much of that time is actually weighted on the weekends; on Saturday and Sunday, we reward ourselves with nearly a whole hour each day.

A quick back-of-the-napkin calculation tells me some shit is wrong here. But with the whole herd of us sliding together, it had essentially blocked my view. Now that I saw it, I was pumped full of resolve.

As corny as it may sound, in my heart I felt the way you do when you follow a friend in a car. Occasionally you might get separated, but you know that somewhere down the line they'll be waiting for you to catch up. They won't forget about you.

But you need to catch up. And then you need to do everything you can to not lose sight of them again.

Now, thanks to that silly article, I had the vehicle to do just that. It felt like every person I'd ever known had read the darn thing, and none of them missed their chance. They all reached out to say "I always knew you were a loser."

Awwww. They missed me, too.

I replied with many versions of "we need to get the band back together" and "it's been too long" and "we need to hang out." I also published a quick follow-up story describing everything that was happening, which triggered a whole new round of correspondence that buried me again. While all this was going on, there was a clear buzz in the media on the entire topic. Loneliness was suddenly hot! Radio interviews came for months. Documentary filmmakers wanted to have conversations. I was booked on a panel about loneliness and happiness at the South by Southwest conference, and it sold out so quickly that a second session was added.

On a personal level, as I made the rounds discussing the original article I was already mentally elsewhere, putting puzzle pieces together to guide me on the next part of the journey. For I truly believed what I had read about loneliness and its consequences. So did the people who wrote to me. Which is why they weren't asking me for more evidence of the cancer. They were asking me for the cure.

The science of loneliness had made its point. Now it was time to see if the science of friendship could do the same.

I made plans, big plans, ridiculous plans, some real and some in my own head. But in the simplest terms, I was taking the steps the experts had advised to get my friend life back on track. And as they'd promised, it was having immediate positive impacts on my emotional health. Simply making plans began to reconnect me with people. Even if our plans never worked out as dreamed, it was good to feel that we still mattered to one another and were working to straighten out the string that connected us.

It's amazing how tangled those strings become when you put them in your pocket and forget about them.

Whether I shall turn out to be the hero of my own friendships or whether I will let them wither and rot—the modern and manly thing to do, it seems—these pages must show.

My quest awaited. I had no way of knowing where it might take me. But I knew exactly where I needed to start: four thousand miles away, on the edge of eastern Europe.

That's because at the very moment I was becoming America's #1 Middle-Aged Loser, I had received a kick straight to the nuts.

As soon as my article was published online, the very first thing I did was send it to Mark and Rory, my buddies from high school, the two guys I had mentioned in the piece.

"Forgot to mention that I wrote a story about how you guys are shitty friends and I miss you," I wrote.

Mark replied right away.

"Who is this?"

That's classic Mark. He communicates almost entirely through ball busting. For years, he's had a standing gag that no matter the company he's with or the situation, if my name comes up, he does this little bit.

"Billy Baker?" he'll ask loudly. "Never liked him."

Then he steers the conversation elsewhere and waits for the pronouncement to make its way back to me.

I saw your friend Mark, or at least I thought he was your friend, but he said he's never liked you.

It's his way of showing me he loves me.

Rory's reply was not funny. "Awesome story," he wrote. "I definitely feel like a loser in this regard."

And then he apologized, because he had failed to mention something kind of important. He had moved.

To Vienna.

I felt blindsided. I tried to swallow the fact, but it got stuck in my throat. One of my two best friends had moved to fucking Austria and hadn't bothered to tell me.

"Something has gone terribly wrong here," I wrote back.

"Terribly wrong," he replied. "We gotta right this ship before it sinks."

Three

In the year 2000, two female scientists at UCLA had an "aha" moment, one that would lead to a breakthrough discovery that forever altered the understanding of how men and women respond to stress. And it all started when one of the women looked around their lab and asked the simple question: Where the fuck did all the guys disappear to?

Her question, which I'm paraphrasing, had already been answered way back in 1915, when a Harvard psychologist by the name of Walter Bradford Cannon coined the term "fight or flight" to describe an animal's response to stress and danger. When an animal feels threatened, the sympathetic nervous system triggers a flood of chemicals that—depending on the situation, the temperament of the organism receiving that cascade of chemicals, and its place in the food chain—leads to aggression or retreat. When the UCLA lab was going through a stressful time, the men all chose the "get the hell out of here" option.

However, most of the early research behind "fight or flight," as well as the subsequent studies that supported Cannon's theory, had one major flaw: They focused almost exclusively on the stress responses of males.

"When the men [in the lab] were stressed, they holed up somewhere on their own," then UCLA scientist Laura Cousino Klein said at the time. This was an easy observation for the female scientists to make because—and here comes the "aha" moment—the women were still in the lab. They hadn't disappeared when the stress hit. Instead, "they came in, cleaned the lab, had coffee, and bonded," Klein noted.

She and a fellow researcher named Shelley Taylor dove into the topic and traced it all back to the hormone oxytocin, which is the cuddliest of all hormones, associated with love and hugging and rainbows and unicorns.

When stress hits the female brain, the pituitary gland, that rather important little pea hanging off the base of the brain, reacts by excreting oxytocin, which counters the urge to fight or flee. Instead, the oxytocin encourages women to gather together and do such things as look after the children, activities that trigger the release of even more oxytocin, and pretty soon everyone's calm and rational and the lab is clean. Klein and Taylor called their theory "tend and befriend."

Men, though, are men. And their response to stress is itself a competition between the most meatheady of body chemicals: testosterone, which wants to fight, and cortisol, which wants to escape. The two work against each other constantly to regulate dominant and competitive behaviors and determine the winner of fight or flight.

I tell you all this to explain a disagreement I had with my wife in the kitchen one day, while I was deciding whether or not to go to Vienna to see Rory. She thought I should go because Rory probably needed a hug and a friend to talk to. I thought what he needed was a slap on the head for screwing town without telling me.

If I'm honest, I must admit that I'm a sucker for those scenes in movies where the guy races off to the airport to save a relationship. They're all the same, but damn if they don't all work. There's the frantic cab ride; the throwing of the money at the driver; the dash into the terminal searching for the departures board; the scanning of the flight numbers; the zoom in on the words "final boarding"; and then . . . the run.

I love the run. The tracking shot. The swelling music. The complete disregard for the fact that you haven't been able to do any of these things in an airport since 9/11. The hero bobbing and weaving his way through the crowds, hurdling children and wheelie bags. Cut to the gate agent, who is announcing the final boarding call. The hero is full-on sprinting now as more children and wheelie bags appear in his path. Now the woman is at the Jetway, taking one last forlorn look over her shoulder, pondering, before hesitantly handing over her ticket, and "Wait . . . !!!" And now I was ready to do all of this for a buddy.

Or was I? The thing was, prior to all this Loserville stuff going down, I had been wondering if I was still friends with Rory. If we hadn't grown apart for a reason. Maybe life had moved on. Maybe we had changed. Maybe we weren't supposed to be close anymore. Maybe, just maybe, there's a reason that "Tell Billy you're moving to Vienna" was not on his list of things to do before he packed.

But there was one thing that stopped me from going all the way with that train of thought, and it was anger. I was angry that he had skipped town without a good-bye. If I didn't care, would I be angry? Would I still be pissed off about what had happened the previous year on our birthdays? Our birthdays are a day apart, and we always celebrated together. Always. Until the previous year, when Rory had "pulled a Rory"—this is a documented term of his coinage—and skipped my fortieth birthday party. Or rather, he "pulled a Rory" by texting me at 11:00 p.m. to say he was just finishing up something and was gonna head to my house, which is like 45 minutes away from his. "Dude, it was a 40th birthday party," I texted back. "Everyone's gone. Asshole."

But here we were—me inside an avalanche as America's #1 Middle-Aged Loser; my best friend on the other side of the world—and it was time again for our birthdays. So I dashed off to the airport to try to save our relationship.

Like I said, I'm a sucker for this kind of stuff. Life is harder when you care.

On the flight, I read a book called *Loneliness*, which was a nice way to assure that the person seated next to me did not try to strike up a conversation. *Loneliness: Human Nature and the Need for Social Connection* was co-written by John T. Cacioppo, a cognitive and social neurologist at the University of Chicago. Before he died in 2018, he was considered the world's leading expert on the science and consequences of loneliness, which he argued were as bad for your health as smoking, obesity, and high blood pressure. This book was perhaps his most prominent work, and it was chock-full of scientifically backed shitty news. This included the haymaker that modern humans seem to be growing lonelier with each succeeding generation. But Cacioppo, to his credit, didn't focus exclusively on the depressing side of things—he also championed the incredible mental and physical health boons of friendship and social connection. I enjoyed those parts of the book so much that I was almost tempted to talk to the guy seated next to me, but that's a known taboo for men. Planes, elevators, and urinals are off-limits for chatting with other men. Just pretend they're invisible. (See: guys, unwritten rules.)

I wasn't really in the mood to talk anyway, because I had a pencil in my hand and I was feeling that good old fight-or-flight chemical battle inside me as I flipped back and forth to page 6, trying to decide whether or not I wanted to go there. For on that page, Cacioppo had printed the questions used in the UCLA Loneliness Scale. First developed in 1978 and revised a couple of times through the years, it's considered the gold standard for empirical studies of the topic. The test consists of 20 quick questions where you rate yourself on a scale from 1 to 4 on queries such as "How often do you feel left out?" and "How often do you feel that people are around you but not with you?" Fun stuff like that. Then you add up your points and get your loneliness "score."

Everyone feels lonely sometimes. That's natural. But now, faced with the idea that I could have a scientific measure of my loneliness, I was straight-up panicking in my seat.

For the past few weeks, ever since my article had appeared, I had been greeted by a constant chorus of "Hey, it's the lonely guy!" It happened enough that I had a practiced response: "I never said I was lonely. I said I was a loser because I don't hang out with the friends I have." It was a glib deflection, which is one of my specialties. But fleeing this topic was clearly not working, so it was time to choose fight. And the first rule of fighting is to know what you're up against—plus it was the day before my birthday and I was in that mood of wispy reflection that comes at the end of each tour of the sun. So I picked up my brand-new pencil—an elegant Blackwing 602 that was an early forty-first birthday gift from my kids, because apparently I'd decided I was old enough to ask for fancy pencils for my birthday—and took the test.

I forced myself to be mortifyingly honest as I rode the feelings that came with each question. Some made me happy. Others triggered a low, guttural "fuuuuuck."

It didn't take very long, and when I was done I added up my points. My loneliness "score" was 44, which just so happened to be the exact average according to a recent study of American adults conducted by the health care company Cigna. But 44 is not "average"—it's the number at which you enter what the scale classifies as "high loneliness."

Scores from 33 to 39 are considered the middle of the spectrum. Normal. Healthy. Rare. Millennials averaged a score of 45.2, meaning that our newest generation of adults is the loneliest in our history. About 71 percent registered as "lonely" to some degree, compared to just half of Baby Boomers.

But the Millennials won't have the lead for long. The generation after them, the young people born after the mid-nineties who are the first to come of age entirely in the era when social life has fused with the digital world and should be in the peak of their friendliest friendship years.

Thus far, 79 percent register as lonely. Their average score is 48.3. This is flat-out horrific.

Before I get to what Rory pulled out of his bag when we met in a cafe in Vienna on the morning of my forty-first birthday—which was the single greatest thing that bastard could have pulled out of his bag in that moment—we need to look back at our history before that moment.

I first met Rory in seventh grade, and we went to high school together, but I never would have described us as close friends. We ran in overlapping crowds, but he was always a bit more "alternative," as they used to say; he liked Morrissey and poetry and wore Doc Martens and flannel. He actually played on the hockey team with Mark and me, though I barely remember it, as he didn't get much ice time and receded into the background in a locker room full of peacocks.

Our first real moment of friendship came at sunrise on a beach in Mexico on the last night of our senior trip, where we shared warm Coronas and impossible dreams for our futures.

Studies show that we tend to choose friends who have qualities we aspire to, and Rory aspired to live a literary life, the sort filled with books and music and pints in pubs. It was a path that was just starting to light up for me, but he was farther along (he had cool older brothers), so I kind of tucked myself under his wing at the beginning. I don't remember the contents of that morning in Mexico that changed our lives. I remember only the recognition that I'd found a mate for masquerading as a writerly type, and the color of the glow that comes off those youthful moments when the world feels freshly yours.

In college we discovered Jack Kerouac and Hunter S. Thompson, which essentially canceled any plans we had to become functioning adults. After graduation we found our way to Dublin, where we rented a grimy top-floor flat in a rough section of the Northside and ran around town with our buddies Patrick and Joe. Together we were all sincerely ambitious and clueless young literary wannabes who read James Joyce and listened to Tom Waits and became maddeningly convinced of it all.

We continued that act back home in an even grimier top-floor apartment just down the street from Harvard Square. And it was there, one night while I was sleeping, that she arrived and everything changed. Let's call her Cersei.

Rory was bartending in the square, and I was working for a tiny neighborhood newspaper while preparing to write the Great American Novel, always vaguely planning and never taking off, as Kerouac would say. Before we knew it, we were approaching our mid-twenties, still charging hard, which meant that one night Rory came stumbling in the door with his usual bullshit, which was to bring the bar home with him after last call.

Now zoom in for a moment and picture 24-year-old Billy Baker jostled awake at 3:00 a.m. on this particular weeknight, testosterone and cortisol fighting it out inside as he decided whether to murder Rory for pulling this shit again or to just get up and join the festivities.

In this episode of Rory's after-hours cafe, the noise woke me before the party even arrived at our apartment, while they were still trying to navigate the final flight of stairs, giggling and shushing and stumbling and tumbling until finally the door opened and the party stepped into the living room, just on the other side of the wall from where I was sleeping. That's when I heard Cersei's voice for the first time.

She began with some condescending compliments on the decor in our living room, like she was impressed we had even made it this far past the Bud Light posters stolen from college bars. She moved on to a snide, unsolicited analysis of the oil portraits of two unknown women we'd acquired through unknown provenance. But she saved her most grandiose soliloquy for the low swivel chairs covered in teal leather that I'd talked Rory into buying in the back of a thrift shop. We called them the Talk Show Chairs, because sitting in them made you feel and act like you were being interviewed on a talk show. We loved those chairs. Everyone loved those chairs. Cersei made it known that she thought otherwise.

The other members of the after-party went crashing through to the kitchen, but Cersei made right for the Talk Show Chairs, and continued talking loudly to Rory down the hall, where he'd gone to fetch drinks. She spoke glowingly of her travels and her art—she was apparently an artist of some sort—and 24-year-old Billy Baker listened from the other side of the painfully thin plaster wall, his entire night of sleep under threat, as a chemical war waged inside his body. Now picture the Billy Baker you would meet two minutes later after he has thrown on some clothes and taken a seat in the other Talk Show Chair. If you're picturing an asshole, a person emitting a cologne that says "it's time to get the fuck out of here," then you would be correct. This is how I met Cersei.

The drinks arrived from the kitchen. I don't remember what we talked about next, but at some point, Cersei stopped, looked at me as though through a monocle, and pronounced, "I don't know what it is, but I just don't like you."

I was, and still am, extremely jealous that she got to say it first.

But I gotta say I appreciated her directness, as I assumed this quick strike would save us a lot of bother and achieve what we both seemed to want, which was to never see each other again.

That's not what happened. No, what happened is that she started dating my best friend. Fifteen years later, our relationship remained roughly where it had started.

Amazingly, my relationship with Rory didn't change as much as I'd feared as they moved from dating to living together to starting a business together. He and I remained partners in crime, and a short time later he came with me to serve as my "photographer" on a ridiculous assignment. I had grown up in South Boston, Massachusetts—that mythical place known as "Southie"—and we traveled to South Boston, Virginia, so I could research a story about why the hell there was a South Boston in Virginia. I never did find the answer, nor did I write the story. Instead, I found a woman named Lori who would become my wife.

Lori and I spent a couple of years in Virginia, and then a couple in New York City, but as our thirties arrived we found ourselves living in the same Cambridge apartment building as Rory and Cersei. It was a funky old place called The London, owned by an all-time character who was mysteriously missing a pinky finger, and for five years Rory and Cersei lived on one side of the first floor and Lori and I lived on the other side of the second. About halfway through Lori and I were joined by our first son, Charlie.

During this period, Cersei and I went through a long stretch of tenuous tolerance, but we never grew to like each other. But Rory seemed to be doing well, and if this was what he wanted, I wasn't going to stand in his way. I never really pried. And that turned out to be a big mistake.

For as he sat across from me in that cafe in Vienna, he told me three big things in rapid succession, things I did not know but should have, because I was supposed to be his best friend.

First, he and Cersei had broken up.

I may have clapped.

Second, he told me he had been in a bad place for much of the time when we'd lost touch.

I stopped clapping.

And last, he told me something I had a tough time grasping: Cersei was in Vienna with him.

They owned a small design firm together, and this European escape had been booked before they broke up, he explained. But he assured me that being in a new place was very good for both of them. It felt like a fresh start, he said.

He proceeded to fill me in on the last stretch of his life, one that I had not been a part of, the solid year or so when I assumed everything was cool because that's what you assume when you haven't seen someone. But everything was not cool.

I was awash with guilt. I had come here thinking Rory was the one who needed a slap for being a shitty friend. It turns out it was me.

But he told me he was better now, and I believed him. And I told him that I was mad that he didn't tell me any of this before, that he should have called me on the tough nights.

This is an easy thing to say in theory, but actually doing it is tricky. I don't know if I would have called him if I'd been in his shoes. Maybe it was because we'd grown apart. Maybe it was because men are taught to not show fear.

It was quiet for a bit before I finally spoke.

"You're wrong about you," I said.

He laughed. Then he did a double laugh, a classic Rory move, though it's more like two squeaks. Then he laughed again, a real deep thank-you-I-needed-that round of squeaks. It was hilarious. Look at us being all serious.

He told me he was ready to move on from everything. To get back to being the old Rory. To get back to being Billy and Rory. To have some fucking fun. To stop talking about all this shit.

He asked me where I was staying, and it turned out that I had rented an apartment just across the courtyard from the one he was renting with Cersei. It was completely random, but I love when shit like that happens. It feels like a beam of light to run your fingers through as it goes by.

That's when Rory stuck his hand inside his bag and announced it was time for our birthday gifts, and he could not have done better for that moment.

I closed my eyes, and when I opened them Rory was holding two Ping-Pong paddles.

"The best thing about Vienna," he announced, "is that for some reason there are public Ping-Pong tables fucking everywhere."

We practically skipped our way through the streets of Vienna, with Rory trying to feel his way to a park he couldn't quite find, as I got my first daylight look at our neighborhood, which sparkled with that marvelous old-Europe patina that will always feel new to the eye of an American. But with this sporting event in front of me, I no longer felt like a wandering tourist but was instead a participant in an important competition. Enough with sitting around talking about this drama. This kid was about to get worked in Ping-Pong.

We found the park gate tucked behind some trees, and inside a nice Ping-Pong table set off in a side nook, just across from the sandbox, where some toddlers were about to be entertained by some trash-talking in a foreign language. This began immediately when Rory revealed something I genuinely did not know about him: He thought he was the shit at Ping-Pong. Which was not possible, because *I* was the shit at Ping-Pong.

Much to my surprise, the cocky prick went point for point with me, through 21 and into overtime, sweating and laughing and cursing each failed put-away. It was so perfect it felt engineered. It may have been the greatest game of Ping-Pong ever played, and it ended with Rory squeaking out a surprising upset. I'm not going to make excuses about jet lag or anything because that's beneath me.

We hit the city and cruised the cathedrals and the palaces and the statues of Mozart and the king with the severe underbite who got down on his knees and asked God to save his people from the plague. We were just two kids acting up and catching up, and it was super. That's a word that Austrian people love, Rory tells me. "Super." It's a good word. It's good when things are super. And everything was super.

Then we met up with Cersei at a symphony concert outside the Nationalbibliothek, and it immediately got cold and drizzly and uncomfortable. I blamed jet lag and turned in early.

That night, as I lay in bed, I recorded in my reporter's notebook this assessment of my relationship with Cersei: It does not work. It has never worked. And there is no reason to spend another minute proving it.

Before I fell asleep, I failed to record what the hell I could or should do about it.

Rory and I met for coffee and Ping-Pong in a new park each morning, trading wins, and then he would head to his apartment to work for a few hours while I explored the city. He and Cersei had built a good little business. She was, in fact, a talented designer, which meant they were constantly in demand and constantly drained by the entire thing, which was mostly unsatisfying. They were both going to be *real* artists, once. Now she spent her time designing restaurant menus and he spent his time shaping "brands" with their clients.

It wasn't what either of them had wanted to be when they grew up. It happens. I'm still planning to write the Great American Novel. I will never write the Great American Novel. What's great about hitting middle age is that you stop pretending the lies you tell yourself are not lies.

Interestingly, when I wrote my original article, a lot of people took issue with a 40-year-old referring to himself as middle-aged. Trust me, it was not something I was desperate to claim, but if I wasn't middle-aged, then I was in no-man's-land. In fact, some models of the stages of life have "young adulthood" lasting until age 40 and "middle age" beginning at 45. The years 40 to 45 are essentially unclaimed. If so, I'm claiming them. Those are the Honest Years. That's when you're finally old enough to be honest. That's when even you become tired of your bullshit.

And Rory was tired of the bullshit. When he'd emerge from it again at the end of each day, alone in that apartment with Cersei, it would take him a few beers to get some lubrication back into his shoulders. He felt free and trapped at the same time. A mortgage and a business will do that to a responsible adult. I didn't know what to tell him. Shit was tangled. We ordered another round. The following day, after beating him at Ping-Pong, I walked to the Alsergrund District for advice.

•   •   •

I arrived at 19 Berggasse, a traditional Viennese apartment building, and a winding staircase brought me to the second floor, where I found a door with a buzzer labeled "Prof. Dr. Freud."

I pressed the button, expecting to be greeted by a receptionist who would ask me to lie uncomfortably on a comfortable sofa while I waited for zee doktor to appear with a meat thermometer that he would stick down into my soul. I've never had terribly warm feelings toward Sigmund Freud, including a memorable run-in during a reading assignment in college that ended with my asking "What did he just say about my mother?"

I'd generally avoided Freud and all things Freudian since, but I was in Vienna, and I believe it was Dr. Freud who said there are no accidents, so I paid a dozen euros to walk around what was once the office and tiny apartment he shared with his wife and six children. The tour comes with free access to the weird thoughts you get while reading weird Freud quotes and looking at photos of the jars where he kept his cocaine.

Did Freud do relationship counseling? How was he on the subject of friendship? Or, for that matter, how were his own friendships? I never read that far, but I have to imagine it would be weird to be friends with Freud. Can you just shoot the shit with him? Does he do ball busting? "How's it hanging, Siggy?" Come to think of it, of the ten or so facts I might be able to rattle off about Freud, one would be that his most famous male friendship, with his protégé and possible guy crush Carl Jung, ended disastrously. There have been a million words spilled over why these two intellectual giants broke up. But I was fascinated by Freud's own words, which he set down in a breakup letter he wrote to Jung that I found reprinted in a book in the gift shop.

Freud was obsessed with the topic of male-male aggression—he called it "the primary hostility"—and he never hid the fact that he was quite good at this aggression himself. He kind of owned it, and his breakup letter was a fairly hostile it's-not-me-it's-you attack on Jung for not fessing up to his own neuroses. "One who while behaving abnormally keeps shouting that he is normal gives grounds for the suspicion that he lacks insight into his illness. Accordingly, I propose that we abandon our personal relations entirely."

Damn, dude. I put the book back on the shelf, thinking I was done fucking with Freud forever, when in that moment my eye was drawn to a limp strip of rubbery blue plastic that was flopping over the side of a small bin nearby. I picked it up, straightened it out, and read the label, which said it was a "psychic ruler." It didn't say what you were supposed to measure. I bought the ruler and got the hell out of there.

As dusk settled on my last evening in Vienna, I took game seven from Rory. Not trying to brag; simply reporting the facts. Our final match took place in a cool little urban park in a neighborhood all the way across town from our apartment building, and we'd trekked there because we were initially thinking we would play the finale in an actual table tennis club. But that club turned out to be a sweaty subterranean room packed with men in unironic short-shorts shouting in German, so we retreated to the fresh air of a nearby park.

After getting crushed in the final, Rory became convinced we were in the same neighborhood where he'd played a bizarre game at a bar. He couldn't remember the names of the game or the bar, but we roamed around forever until at last we found the game. It's called nailing, and it involves raising a hammer high and then attempting to drive a nail as deep into a log of wood as possible. It's much more difficult than it sounds. Especially once the schnapps becomes involved. Loser buys a round each time, and it turned out I was not a natural at nailing, so I spent the last of my euros on cinnamon-flavored gasoline.

We'd had a great week, but as I waited in the predawn for a taxi to the airport, I felt strange just leaving it like that. I was going to hop on a plane and Rory was going to return to being alone in a foreign country with the chief source of his unhappiness? He and Cersei were due to come home in a few weeks, but this felt like the definition of insanity, doing the same thing over and over and expecting a different outcome. While that quote is often misattributed to Albert Einstein, it appears instead to have come from a pamphlet printed in the 1980s by Alcoholics Anonymous. Which makes sense; they know a thing or two about such things.

The sun began to rise as my taxi made its way to the airport, and I allowed myself a peaceful moment to appreciate what I had accomplished during the week. Never before had I shown such naked intent in a friendship. I'd flown across a good chunk of the planet to stop the skid in its tracks. That meant something to both of us. We were good. Definitely good.

I had done something men are not supposed to do. I had put myself in a vulnerable position, and it had been rewarded. The old me would have stayed home and played it cool and just told Mark that Rory was an asshole. And that person would have had one fewer friend.

I was ready to push onward. Step two was already in the works, and it was the opposite of playing it cool. In fact, it was hard to think of anything as uncool as trying to get the band back together to redo the best day of high school.

Four

A week after I returned from Vienna, I was sitting alone in a beach chair along the foul line of a softball field at 9:54 a.m. on a Friday, shitting bricks. I cracked open a beer, looked toward the heavens, and promised to be good from now on to whoever might be listening.

I glanced again toward the parking lot, hoping, pleading, already embarrassed to the point of nausea. I poured the beer into a red plastic cup, the world's worst camouflage, just to give myself something to do as I tried my best to look nonchalant and relaxed. It was still early. I had said 10:00 a.m. No one would dare to arrive on time, right?

By 10:01 a.m., I was ready to puke. If I wanted to go back to high school, I had gotten my wish, because my body was riddled with awkwardness and insecurity. *What was I thinking?* Well, I'll tell you what I *had* been thinking, back when I thought this was a good idea. Who am I kidding, I thought it was a superstar champagne genius idea. But that felt like a million miles away now. I was thoroughly convinced that this was a terrible idea. One of my worst, and there's strong company there.

So what I had been thinking was that I missed my high school friends, which is lame-o city. And I'm not talking about the people I was still friends with (though it's not like I was hanging out with them on the regular). I meant everyone. The whole messy lot. Listen, I know the thought of high school gives many people terrible flashbacks, but I have fond memories of those years. Or maybe I've just blocked out all the painfully awkward stages the brain and body tumble through during that tight period of time.

Either way, this whole friendship quest had me thinking a lot about my high school classmates. Deep down, I felt a strange desire to be around those people who knew the old me, the long me, the me that has no use for pretending that I'm profoundly different now that I'm an adult because they knew the dumpster fire I was as a teenager. They know my shit. And I know theirs. It's hard to play it cool when they can all just say, "Remember the time the girls tied you to a pole on the bus and left you there?"

In studies, when people are asked to name their "best friend," they typically choose someone from childhood or high school. They do this even if they rarely see that person and are measurably closer to newer friends. There's a reason for this: There's just something solid about being able to say, "We go back together." I feel like I'm still great friends with those girls who tied me to the bus, even though I hadn't seen them in years. They know me better than the people who sit next to me in my office and see me every day. And it felt important at this moment to let my guard down and reach back in time and say I still wanted to be friends with the people I knew during the phase in life when you never let your guard down and say such things. If I was going to fix my friendship problem, my gut told me to start from the ground up and see what happened.

Which led me to this moment of high school awkwardness, sitting alone in that park, like I was sitting alone in the cafeteria. And I had arrived at that moment by asking myself a ridiculous question: If I could relive one day from high school, one feeling of juvenile togetherness when we were all in cahoots against the adult world, what would it be? The answer was crystal clear: Senior Skip Day.

I'm pretty sure every senior class does, or at least attempts to do, a skip day. It's an institutionalized act of faux rebellion, and there's no one who thinks they're more rebellious than a high school senior, especially during that period at the end of the school year when you think you've outrun all the things the administration can do to your "permanent record." Everyone believes their senior class is the most originally rebellious group in teenage history. It's only when you're older that you realize the adults have seen it a million times and don't really care. Instead, they go through the motions of sternness so as to provide the critical aspect of rebellion, which is having something to rebel against. No one is more ready for a school year to end than a teacher. Ever seen a teacher during the first week of summer vacation? Happiest fucking person on earth.

It's hard to find that soft and silly feeling of pretend group rebellion as an adult, but I was convinced I had hit on it. And so on the day before I boarded my flight to Vienna, feeling myself already sliding down into that optimist's pit that comes from committing to being vulnerable, I asked myself "What's the worst that can happen?" and pulled up the Facebook page for my high school class. After taking about 87 deep breaths and pacing around the room, I finally sat down and went for it.

"Senior Skip Day for the Class of '93 is coming back! Daisy Field. Friday. May 19. 10 a.m. Yes, it's on a Friday. That's the whole point. You have to skip. Remember how good it feels to just say FUCK IT and skip?" I really did write "FUCK IT" in capital letters. I already told you I was a loser.

The post was seen by 144 people, about half of my graduating class. Some left comments. Some hit "like." There were lots of definitely maybes. And when all was said and done, I hadn't a clue if a single one of them was actually coming.

At 10:08 a.m. I opened another beer. There had been no sign of activity in the parking lot. Every dog walker or runner who came by lifted and then crushed my spirits. I spent some time writing in my reporter's notebook, just to look like I was doing something other than panicking, and recorded that the weather was perfect. May in New England had thus far been doing a wonderful impression of November, but on this day the temperature was about 80 and the birds were chirping and the flowers were blooming and I was feeling that spring amnesia that is necessary to survive living somewhere that freezes solid for so much of the year. "Today is a 'get me out of the office day,'" I recorded optimistically, because I had nothing else to record. "Today just screams 'skip.'"

10:15 a.m. Nothing. Metamorphosis is supposed to be painful, right?

10:21 a.m. Scanning the horizon for a building to jump off.

10:25 a.m. Wait, hold on. Someone was walking across the field toward me. I tried not to get too excited, but there was something about their gait. They seemed awkward and nervous, like they were trying to remember how to walk normally. I tried to act casual, though I couldn't remember what I normally did with my hands, so I abandoned that and squinted across the field until a tall, redheaded woman came into focus. Is that . . . ? Yes. Yes, it is.

I leapt out of my chair and way too enthusiastically hugged this girl who was not exactly a close friend of mine in high school but was in that moment my Best Friend in the World. We stumbled through all the nervous pleasantries—"It's great to see you." "You look great." "What are you up to nowadays?"—and then another person came walking across the field, and soon another, and then another. I swear they had been hiding in the bushes, unwilling to make the first move. Soon there was an actual crowd. When the dust had settled and the pleasantries were done and the nervous energy had exited through my fingertips, two dozen responsible adults, including a couple who were supposed to be teaching at that very moment, decided to say FUCK IT and skip and go drink a beer or two at the park where we used to go act up on half days.

What made it so special was that every single person who had shown up had been willing to be vulnerable, to walk across that field and announce that they too would enjoy something like this. They had announced to the world, "It's been too long!" They had shown intent, which was emerging more and more as such a simple and important thing in this quest. Studies show we like people more if we know they like us. Skipping out on life to go play with their high school friends demonstrates that these relationships still matter to their history and maybe even to their present.

Once we all loosened up and the nerves had drifted away and the day settled into what it was going to be, a few people brought up my article. "We're the people who know you actually *were* a loser sitting alone in the cafeteria," one of the women said.

Awwwww. It had definitely been too long.

I forgot to mention what had happened the day before Senior Skip Day. You're not going to believe this shit.

I was standing in front of the dugout on a Little League baseball field, surrounded by a mob of seven- and eight-year-old boys, each of them demanding something from me in a high-pitched squeal.

"Can I pitch?"

"I want to catch."

"You said I could pitch!"

"Can I dab if I get a hit?"

These were the last words I would ever hear in stereo.

I had somehow ended up as the coach of my son Charlie's baseball team, an offer I had accepted only to protect the kids from the adults who do their best to ruin youth sports. What I did not anticipate was that trying to keep everyone else from being worked up left me constantly worked up. And at this moment, all worked up and surrounded by squealing children, I felt a small pop in my right ear.

I really didn't think too much about it. I assumed a piece of wax had become lodged in there—because I couldn't hear anything at all—and resumed yelling at children in my effort to keep other adults from yelling at children. When the game was over, I drove to the drugstore and bought some ear wax removal drops, which did nothing, but I really didn't sweat it because the following day was Senior Skip Day. It was probably an ear infection, I told myself, and spent much of Senior Skip Day asking people to repeat what they'd just said because I had some sort of ear infection.

The first two doctors I went to agreed that it was probably an ear infection. They were wrong. When I finally went to see a specialist—two weeks later, after the ear infection treatments had done nothing—he spent about half a second looking into my ear before informing me I did not have an ear infection. He then wrote something on a piece of paper and handed it to me.

"This is what I think you have," he said as I looked down at the piece of paper.

There were just three words on the page, in surprisingly plain English for a medical diagnosis.

"Sudden Hearing Loss."

The doctor then sat across from me and said, "You're a reporter. Now ask me some questions."

"Am I going to get my hearing back?"

"I'm optimistic," he said in a tone that was not too optimistic, then went about asking me how things were going at the *Boston Globe* like we were just two guys sitting at the bar, shooting the breeze about the future of print journalism. Did this guy just say I was permanently deaf in my right ear? That can happen? You can just lose your hearing in a split second?

After many more specialists and painful injections straight

through my eardrum, plus a straight month where I spent two hours a day in a hyperbaric oxygen chamber in a last-ditch effort to save some hearing, the answer was yes. Yes, you can lose your hearing in a split second. And it had happened to me.

What's kind of funny is that just before all this I had read an article in the *New Yorker* about the prevalence of hearing loss in the United States—37 million adults apparently have some form of it. One statement that stood out to me, for obvious reasons, was that "hearing loss can lead to social isolation," which can make aging "seem worse than it already is."

I had shelved hearing loss away in the "things to research" section of my brain, alongside the neurons that were to remind me to examine all the social obstacles older Americans faced as they suffered through an epidemic of loneliness. Those files were hidden behind a more pressing matter, which was figuring out how to make friendship work for me. Yet in an instant, standing on that Little League field being yelled at by frothing second graders, I had skipped ahead two generations.

Hearing loss sucks. I can confirm this. True, there are many, many worse things that can happen to you in an instant. It's not cancer. Instead, it's a constant source of annoyance and frustration. Restaurants are a nightmare. Theaters. Gyms. Arenas. Really anywhere we typically have social gatherings. If I couldn't situate myself in such a way where I could put the world on my left side, I found myself in an aural nightmare that would quickly turn my aggravation levels to 11. I was constantly asking everyone around me to repeat themselves. And if I'm honest, I was in a constant state of melancholy as I processed that this was a permanent problem. What saved me was the whimsical idea that it was some challenge thrown down to me from the gods, a well-placed social obstacle for the asshole who had just declared he was going to be the hero of his own friendships.

If the universe was gonna hit me with old-guy problems, then it was worth looking at some old-guy solutions.

On my first "Wednesday Night" with Mark and Rory, we got into the car and immediately reverted to teenagers.

"Where do you want to go?"

"I don't know; where do you want to go?"

This went on for a comically long stretch of time, the three of us driving around aimlessly, just kind of hanging out, which was the plan anyway. But we still felt like we had to actually do something, so we ended up at a newish mall just outside the city because it had free parking and we are old.

It's not that I wanted anything in particular to happen on that first Wednesday Night—just the opposite. It was only a few days after my hearing diagnosis, which I was still processing, and what I really needed to happen was nothing. A couple of hours of nothing.

What Mark thought I needed was getting my balls busted through the roof.

We went to dinner, and Mark immediately apologized to the waitress for his deaf friend. He had her shout the specials at me. Rory, just back from Vienna, pretended to use sign language. There were more apologies for the deaf friend. Mark told the waitress he had never liked me anyway.

• • •

The mall became our thing on Wednesday night. It was a running joke. Sometimes we did something crazy like go bowling, or catch a movie, or grab ice cream. You can do everything at a mall!

Rather quickly, the whole thing fizzled. The intent was there, and stronger than ever. Those silly little nights of going to hang with your friends just to hang with your friends felt amazing. But pretty soon another Wednesday at the mall wasn't strong enough to fend off the life intrusions. The kids had games. There was work bullshit. Et cetera. Et cetera. There was talk of finding an actual activity to participate in. We even made a visit to the local table tennis club before realizing those dudes were ultraserious and we were in over our heads, so we left without playing a game and drove to our mall, as we'd come to call it.

After about two months, Wednesday Night had mostly run its course. It was clear that we valued our friendships more than ever, but in a lesson in actually making it work, we had failed. We had neglected the fundamental rule of male friendship. Intent was the gesture, but activity was the glue. And as crazy as it is to say, I had no clue what we should do.

I spent my Wednesdays alone for a while, reading up on some basic questions I had about friendship, riddles that needed to be answered if I was going to find some larger way forward. Like, for starters, why do we need friends? If we can survive without them, then why do we still crave them?

"First agriculture, and then industry, changed two fundamental things about the human experience," Sebastian Junger points out in *Tribe*, which is an extended argument in favor of tribal living. "The accumulation of personal property allowed people to make more and more individualistic choices about their lives, and those choices unavoidably diminished group efforts toward a common good. And as society modernized, people found themselves able to live independently from communal groups. A person living in a modern city or a suburb can, for the first time in history, go through an entire day—or an entire life—mostly encountering complete strangers. They can be surrounded by others and yet feel deeply, dangerously alone."

John Cacioppo, the late loneliness expert at the University of Chicago, spoke often about how loneliness triggered a physical pang, like hunger or thirst, and that it was the *feeling* of loneliness that did such damage to the body. So does that make friendship a basic need like food and water? If so, why?

In 1943, the American psychologist Abraham Maslow published his famous theory about what drives humans. He mapped it out on a pyramid, known as "Maslow's hierarchy of needs," and at the base of the pyramid he uses the term "physiological" to describe the most fundamental needs, such as food, water, shelter, sleep, and sex. Above that is safety, and then "belonging and love" (sometimes called "social needs"), followed by esteem. Working from the bottom, an individual must mostly satisfy these four basic layers, which Maslow called "deficiency needs," or risk appearing physically well but suffering from an internal anxiety and tension. Until those base levels are satisfied, a person will feel discouraged and lack the motivation to pursue the higher-level needs at the top of the pyramid, the fifth level that Maslow called "self-actualization."

But if food, water, and shelter are accounted for, and probably cable and Internet, why do we still need others to achieve self-actualization and turn off the rumbling hum of anxiety and stress?

And how many friends do we need? There are old aphorisms about how if you have one friend you have more than most, but every study I see on reaping the full health and happiness benefits of this magical supplement speaks more in terms of a robust social circle. But how many friendships can we realistically maintain within the constraints of time and brainpower and looking for shoes?

Also, while I was at it, why are women allegedly better at this than men?

They were funky questions. Funkier still was that they seemed to be leading to the same source. It was all in the hips.

Five

I stood on the top deck of a cruise ship, looking down at a stage set up next to the swimming pool, which was at that moment surrounded by three thousand ex–teenage girls who were collectively vibrating like a hive. We had just shoved off from the port of New Orleans, and as we motored down the Mississippi River I was doing my best to settle in and accept what already felt like maybe not the best idea I'd ever had. That's when an Australian woman named Jo came marching toward me.

She had been standing with a small group of women about a dozen feet to my left, and I could sense they were talking about me. If I were them, I would have been talking about me, too.

Jo approached, sized me up quickly, and hit me with a question I suspected I might have to answer a few times in the next four days.

"Why are *you* here?" she said.

She asked in a way that felt more curious than suspicious, which I appreciated, for there were several ways to interpret the clear fact that I did not fit the standard demographic of passengers on the New Kids on the Block cruise.

Why *was* I there? The shortest answer is that I wanted to experience a Girls Trip, which is perhaps the most celebrated act in modern American friendship. But my anthropological ambition came with a basic catch: The presence of a guy on a Girls Trip would negate the sacredness of the event. The only way it would work is if I had the power of invisibility. Which seemed impossible until I learned that the New Kids on the Block had an annual cruise.

This discovery felt like a hole in the matrix, an opportunity to experience hundreds of Girls Trips simultaneously with low risk of contamination because I was not a New Kid on the Block, so they would give zero fucks about me. I had recently been to see the New Kids at Fenway Park, and not since tenth grade had I felt so invisible to women. It was a sight to behold. They even took over the men's room like a storming army, and when the line for the stalls became too long I watched a woman back herself in like a truck and answer once and for all the question: Can a woman pee in a urinal? She clearly did not care, because I clearly did not matter. It was like I wasn't even there. The only guys who mattered were named Jordan, Joey, Donnie, Danny, and Jon.

This seems like as good a time as any to pause and examine the story of human evolution. It's a story that spans millions of years, and I'm not going to pretend to understand every detail of how an ape in a tree became a modern human who complains that bathrooms on airplanes are too small.

Instead, I'm going to focus on the problem created by two of our greatest evolutionary "advantages": bipedalism and big-brainism.

Bipedalism was a nice improvement, because walking on two feet freed the hands for important uses, like texting while driving. And standing upright lifted our eyes up to a height where we had a better view of all the shit in the grass that was desperate to kill the wimpy creatures who had just abandoned the safety of the trees.

The big brain is of more questionable value if you pause for even a tiny second and look at what we've wrought with it, but that's a conversation for another day. What I'm here to discuss is something inarguable, which is the weight distribution problem created by that disproportionately heavy skull sitting atop this newly erect creature.

To support the bipedal transport of that big brain, the scaffolding of the body needed to evolve to lower the center of gravity. To accomplish this, the pelvis narrowed significantly. This was all fine and good except for one minor problem, which was when one of those increasingly larger heads had to be squeezed out of increasingly smaller hips during childbirth. It's the simple reason why humans have more birth complications than other apes.

To solve this problem, human females adapted by giving birth earlier, when the head of the baby is smaller. That earlier due date gave both the child and mother a better chance of surviving the birth, but it meant that a human baby is born premature when compared to other animals, completely defenseless and unable to survive on its own, with vital systems still under development. They're useless for years. Some still live at home into their thirties.

For our female ancestors, giving birth successfully was just the first step toward passing down their genes, which is the real evolutionary goal of any organism. But to ensure that their offspring would survive long enough to produce their own offspring, women also needed a strong social circle. Forming bonds with others became the key to basic survival, a behavior that would enhance the frequency with which women's genes were passed on to future generations.

It's also the story of why we have friends.

Imagine, if you will, that you're a primitive woman trying to raise a newborn in that harsh world before the era of parenting blogs. You're going to need a network for those days when your full-time job is keeping the child alive, but that shouldn't be a problem because prior to that you probably spent much of your time contributing to the gathering and preparing of food. The social joys of making a meal with friends are known to all who have done so. And as research into modern hunter-gatherer tribes shows, the most accurate and efficient foraging occurs in large, communicating teams of socially bonded individuals.

Long story short, social skills were a biological necessity for women.

Meanwhile, the men were out hunting, an activity that requires an awful lot of silence.

Trading favors, the relationship tit for tat that social scientists call reciprocal altruism, was long thought to be the basic backbone of friendship. But recent research has revealed that we actually care less about "fairness" with our friends than we do when dealing with strangers or acquaintances. In a friendship, when either person insists on repaying a favor it's seen as signaling a weakness in the relationship. Friendship is what happens beyond the tracking of favors. One study gave pairs of friends and pairs of strangers a task and told them the reward would be divided by contribution. The strangers used different-colored pens to make tracking easier. The friends just agreed to split the reward. Among the traits exclusive to *Homo sapiens*, altruism and selflessness are near the top of what makes us human.

Which leads to the alliance hypothesis, devised by Peter DeScioli and Robert Kurzban, which argues that friendship is at least partly about assembling a squad for potential conflicts. Every one of your ancestors survived long enough to reproduce a surviving offspring, and they did this successfully in every single era of human history, unbroken, or else you wouldn't be here right now. You come from a line of some tough motherfuckers. But now that basic survival has become infinitely easier, there's a big evolutionary catch for men: What do we do with that long stretch of our genetic code that was selected for aggression and competition? What do we do with those chemicals the rest of the time, especially once we've mated and fulfilled our basic obligation to our genes?

To that I ask you: Have you ever been around a group of guys strapping something to the roof of a car? All of a sudden everyone's an expert on aerodynamics and the load-bearing capacities of knots.

Ever been around a campfire with a group of guys when someone gets up to put on a log? Well, I can assure you, wherever he puts it is the wrong place. Hell, the real man's man will insist it didn't need another log just yet.

Have you met the overly firm handshake guy? Coming in hard with the eye contact? I was recently introduced to another dad at a ball game, and this prick nearly broke all eight carpal bones in my hand. *Nice to meet you. Let's never hang out.*

The overly firm handshake is the classic example of the "man's man," who is a much more toxic species than the "guy's guy." Where the man's man sees other males as competition, the guy's guy sees them as companions. No male falls all the way in one direction or the other, and it's often the company or the situation that dictates where on the spectrum our actions land.

Once, I helped organize a "guys' night" for my gym, inspired by the female members who have "ladies' night" every Monday, when they do a workout and then go to a Mexican restaurant. Our plan was to eat wings and drink a couple of beers and then go bowling. About a dozen guys came, and it was going well until a "man's man" decided that bowling was lame and announced that we should go to a strip club. No one was interested, but the man persisted and persisted, and soon the peer pressure won out and everyone was piling into cars and going somewhere they clearly didn't want to go, lest they be considered less of a man.

I stood on the curb and watched them drive away. I'd already been to my last strip joint. I guess I'm not a man's man. (Interestingly, we have never had a "guys' night" again.)

You know what's the lamest part of the whole "man's man"

act? That it's just that: an act, a performance, some attempt to behave in a way that fits a fictional character, the "real man," the "manly man." And that man is nearly always portrayed as a loner, a "man against the world." The reality is that there are no successful loners in the history of social evolution. Being a solo survivalist is arduous and inefficient. Survival has only been accomplished in groups.

I try to be a "guy's guy." But I'd be lying if I didn't admit that I can flip into the "man's man" caricature on a moment's notice. It gives you false rationalization for aggression, however slight. Like most men who've made it into the Honest Years, I've mostly grown past the stage where aggression is a part of daily life.

That's not to say competition no longer occurs. That shit isn't going anywhere, but at my age it has shifted to ideas. If he can't present a better idea, the "man's man" can simply belittle the idea presented. I've uttered the words "the fire doesn't need another log just yet." It's an exhausting facade to uphold, always policing, always protecting some ideal, always demanding proficiency in adherence to some invisible and unnecessary code. It's an awful lot of work to undermine joy and togetherness.

Where a "man's man" communicates with criticism, a "guy's guy" communicates with ball busting, which is a compliment disguised as criticism. It's a safe deflection, still masculine, and while I don't have a direct figure on how many of the meaningful interactions in my life have come in the form of ball busting, I suspect that it is high. That sounds awful, but I'm quite proud of this fact, for ball busting can occur only among friends. In any other situation it is indeed criticism. When a buddy gives another buddy shit for the way he tied a couch to the roof of the car, it's nothing but love.

I grew up in South Boston, in the old Southie, a place that no longer exists and feels almost fictional because Hollywood has made so many damn movies about it. But it was indeed real, and even stranger than fiction, and in that alternate reality I used to run around the neighborhood with a pack of kids who hung around a schoolyard and could easily number 50 or 60. Inside the pack, social life was dog-eat-dog—you were either busting balls or having your balls busted. So I became more than capable at wielding a verbal ice pick to defend or attack. I could hold my own with most anyone, though there was a guy in my crew we called Stubba who could make you wish you'd never been born. He still destroys me every time I run into him, which typically involves his making jokes about my mother, which is great because it means we're still friends.

At its core, ball busting is a friendly form of humor, and that is vitally important. Because laughter, dance, and music are three things that humans make that other animals do not. Each of them is believed to have existed even before language, and they are incredibly time-efficient methods to accomplish what scientists call social grooming. You can share an endorphin hit with many people at once, rather than the one-on-one required of physical touch. Our social groups are much larger than other primates', and we've got too many things to do and people to see to sit around combing one another's hair like they do.

For men, ball busting and laughter can provide a safe distance from, and path to, the intimacy that topics of emotional honesty require. It can also afford a direct, if somewhat hidden, way to bring up topics that women actually shy away from addressing head-on. A landmark study on "conversational coherence" looked at pairs of same-sex friends at various ages, from second grade to young adults. The friends sat in chairs talking, and were studied for the congruence of their physical alignment and topic cohesion. The girls and women were "more physically still, more collected into the space they inhabit, more directly aligned with each other through physical proximity, occasional touching, body posture, and anchoring of eye gaze," wrote Deborah Tannen, the author of the study.

The boys basically did the opposite. Where the girls were turned toward one another and focused on the concerns of one, the boys sat parallel and had parallel concerns. They only touched in playful aggression.

But that doesn't mean the men were less engaged. The girls liked to gossip about others. Dislike of a third person is a well-established form of human bonding. Admit it—there really is nothing like the tingly feeling of coming conspiracy you feel toward someone in the moment they take a sly look around to make sure the coast is clear before they dish the dirt.

However, if the boys in the experiment had something to say about someone, it was usually "aimed directly at his friend who is present." In this sense, Tannen argued, they were more direct. But I've gotta wonder how much of that was done behind the safety of ball busting.

I'm coming to a point here, and it involves ball busting as an outlet for male aggression, and the reason I was on the New Kids on the Block cruise. And it goes back to those big three tools humans use for social grooming in groups: laughter, dance, and music.

Ball busting, however, contains a fundamental flaw, one that has done immeasurable harm to the male psyche, and basically eliminated dance and music as potential outlets for bonding.

That is the use of the term "gaaay."

It's a form of self-policing, some fucked-up safe word that got called out if any behavior approached a level where it felt intimate or affectionate. Really anything that felt "feminine," and that list was long.

It was not used to describe romantic attraction to another man—though it certainly insulted that entire idea in an inexcusable way—but instead was used to reinforce what Niobe Way, a psychology professor at NYU, calls the "crisis of connection" among men. We so fear being called *gaaay* for making connections that are "feminine" that we sacrifice intimacy for casual banter.

It's a huge disconnect, perhaps the central one at the heart of the problems with modern male bonding. And unlike many "male" things, it cannot be blamed on genetics. It's cultural. It's learned.

And when I was a kid, singing and dancing were definitely on the girls list, which was the "gay" list, which meant the New Kids were totally gay, and for a boy to admit to liking the New Kids on the Block was like the gayest thing you could do.

So why was I on the cruise, Jo? It was tough to say. I was piecing it all together.

. . .

Of course, I told the Australian woman none of that as she questioned me on the top deck of the cruise ship. She was suspicious enough, and had I informed her I was here because of women's hips, she might have called in the Navy SEALs. Instead, I told her something that was also true, which is that I was there to write an article about the enduring cult of New Kids on the Block fans. I'd convinced an editor that this was a worthy story because it most certainly was; the whole thing is rather endearing, when you stop and think about following a teenage crush into middle age. But the chief reason I had pitched the story was to get access to this huge laboratory of women socializing free of the male gaze.

Yet as I looked down at the buzzing hive of women waiting for the New Kids to appear on the stage, I had already begun to question what I was realistically hoping to see from women that I had not already witnessed. I'm not claiming to be an expert on women, but I'm not inexperienced either.

"You're definitely in for something," Jo informed me. "You're going to see women do some shit you've never seen before."

I was relieved to hear that, because if I'm honest, there was something naïve in me that believed that if I just approached the scene as though I were wearing a pith helmet and a monocle, I would learn something valuable that I could snatch and bring back to the boys' cabin.

Jo and her crew were exactly what I was expecting to find

on the cruise, a squad of 40-something moms who were in on the joke. She told me that she and her friends came nearly every year—this was the ninth annual cruise—and acted silly, and crushed on their teenage crushes, and replayed happy memories and made some new ones. It all seemed perfectly harmless, which only revived my fear that I'd made a major miscalculation if I believed women on a Girls Trip would behave radically differently than they did when there were men around.

Then Donnie Wahlberg's voice came over the speakers, and a jolt of energy raced through the crowd. I swear it was like the place got hit by lightning. Donnie, I would soon learn, does most of the talking for the New Kids, and he led everyone through an oath they apparently do at the start of each cruise. The oath sounded like it was written by a college freshman going through a New Agey phase, and you were supposed to repeat every line after him, and all the lines seemed to end with the word "love," and the whole thing went on too long.

When it was finally over, Donnie lowered his voice into a snarl and said, "This is the real motherfucking love boat." And then it went off. The women let go. And I'm talking *let go*.

The simplest explanation of what happened is that all the women started dancing together, which is something American men don't do because it's gaaay. This dumb decision deprives males of perhaps the single greatest driver for "collective effervescence," which is that exhilaration and euphoria you receive from being in a group of people joined by a common purpose. It has "a sort of electricity," according to Émile Durkheim, the French sociologist who coined the term in the early twentieth century. The feeling is defined as more of a connecting flow, warmly enveloping people and lifting them to a feeling that more than a few people find spiritual. And it works like superglue for a group. Every culture and religion does it. And needs it.

American men do not dance. Occasionally at weddings. Never at New Kids on the Block cruises. Always for some reason fighting off what Bronwyn Tarr at Oxford University describes as our natural human tendency to synchronize our movements. We often tap our fingers together or nod our heads to some shared rhythm, and that joint mimicry opens up all kinds of feel-good chemicals we use to meld self with other.

Below me on the ship, I could practically feel the charge coming off that synchronicity. Then the New Kids on the Block walked onto the stage, and the crowd turned into a full-on blur. Durkheim coined "collective effervescence" in an attempt to explain the loss of individuality approaching the spiritual that could happen in those moments. Religion, he believed, came from directing the great positive energy created during collective effervescence toward some sort of totem, which becomes sacred. In this case, that totem was a boy band consisting of five middle-aged dads.

The New Kids on the Block are no longer kids. They were all closer to 50 than 40. But I must give them credit, as they have certainly put in the effort to stay boy-band pretty. Ain't no one been fucking with carbs with the cruise coming up. As they prowled the small stage, letting the ladies get their first look at the merchandise, each of the Kids made the unmistakable declaration that his shirt was definitely coming off at some point between here and Cozumel.

There would be time for the shirts to come off later. This was just the welcome show—the tease for the show coming up that night. And then the party after that. And then the after-party after that. On repeat, on a boat, on the Gulf of Mexico, with no escape.

Four days later, at 4:23 a.m., I stepped out of an elevator and walked toward the stage next to the pool. Moments earlier, I had woken up in my small cabin in a panic, as I discovered that the "quick nap" I intended to take before the final night's festivities had lasted roughly eight hours. I could have slept eight more. But I dragged myself out of bed and up to the after after-party because, as Holden Caulfield once said, sometimes you just need a good-bye.

It had been a Girls Trip on steroids, and I was hoping to spend the final night drawing up some grand conclusion, if there was one to be had, about females and friendship. This was a dangerous idea, for one should never force epiphanies, especially when they involve generalizations about women. As I've said before, the only thing I know for certain about women is that they don't want a man telling them how they think or feel.

Yet there was no question that my near invisibility had yielded some observations worth pondering. The first discovery was that the women I spoke with were not really there for the New Kids on the Block. They definitely loved the band. But the reason they had come on a New Kids on the Block *cruise* was because it was utterly ridiculous. I've always admired this about groups of women; they seem more likely to choose something fun, even if it means sacrificing the sacred act of "playing it cool." It's the reason a bachelorette party looks very different from a bachelor party.

As I arrived at the stage in the predawn light, only about a third of the women, and two of the New Kids, were still standing, all of them admirably committed to the idea that the party wouldn't stop until the ship bumped the pier in New Orleans.

I backed out of the action, which was as sloppy as one might expect at this late hour, and again climbed the stairs to what had become my observation post on the top deck. There I took one last look at the absurd view, for it was a view that contained so much to admire about women.

Below me were many "whoo girls," and "whoo girls" are great. If you aren't familiar with the term, it's used to describe a pack of women who are behaving in such a manner that you're likely to hear one or two or hundreds of "whoos" shouted into the air. It's not necessarily a term of flattery, and it's basically deployed like the female equivalent of "bro," used to mock any group of same-sex friends who dare to exhibit signs that they're having a good time. Such things have been deemed unacceptable, in case you haven't heard.

For four days, I studied these whoo girls diligently, looking for some social secrets, the monocle tight to my eye. But I found nothing new. No, what I found was something obvious, sitting there in front of me, which felt embarrassingly revelatory, less a secret of women than a blind spot for me. It was the dancing. These women danced their asses off. They danced waiting for drinks at the bar. They danced waiting to pee. They danced while loading up their plates at the cruise ship buffet. Each night, they got dressed up in whatever the theme was and danced all night at the pool party. I'm putting the average at three or four hours of dancing per day, and that's on top of all the singing, for they sang along with every song, always at the tippity-top of their lungs. When we were leaving our very brief shore excursion in Cozumel, I walked behind a crew of four women on the remarkably long pier leading back to the ship, and they danced and sang the whole time, hooting and hollering at everyone to join them, four moms with mortgages who were consumed with the whole damn thing.

If the world is run by very simple principles, then singing and dancing as a means for human bonding is an easy one to decipher. "We humans are a musical species no less than a linguistic one," as Oliver Sacks put it. But that didn't mean I had found anything to steal and take back to the boys' camp. It couldn't be singing, could it? Unless the point was to get laid, singing was firmly shelved as gaaay, but nowhere near as gaaay as getting the fellas together to dance. That one is 100 percent off-limits. I wouldn't even know where to start. Um, instead of the mall, do you guys want to go dancing?

Only twice in my life have I ever seriously danced with other guys. Once was when I learned a dance with the groomsmen for a buddy's wedding. And the other was when I was 11, for the end-of-summer lip-sync contest, when four buddies and I burned through a VHS tape of the New Kids on the Block performing

"My Favorite Girl" and then drilled the dance routine until we had it dead. We did not do this because it was absurdly fun and the best thing we did as friends all summer. Der.

No, we did it because we were making fun of the New Kids for being so gaaay. How are you not getting this?

Six

This next experiment felt like a slam dunk, and it started when my buddy Nick heard me talking about all this stuff on a radio show and shot me an email. "The topic hit home with me big-time," he wrote. "I sometimes feel like George Clooney in *Up in the Air*. I'm surrounded by people but feel that I have no friends."

He confessed that he had just skipped a wedding and bachelor party for a good friend. Both involved getting on a plane to a far-off destination, and with four kids at home he had used the valid excuse that he didn't have the money.

"But," he wrote, "I am miserable with the feeling that I should have wanted to go more."

Something about that statement crushed me, because I knew it all too well.

Nick had been a close friend of mine in the period right after college, when his crew of high school friends merged with my crew in those years of shitty apartments and shitty relationships and shitty jobs that are pretty much the best years ever. We met one summer at the end of college when both of our crews somehow ended up working at a snooty golf course, and we bonded over our shared ability to shit all over the rich dicks we caddied for.

Nick said that his best friends in the town where he lived were his cycling friends. "We meet at 6 a.m. and bomb around real quick to be home before 7. We joke that we don't even know which of us is bald or not because we never see each other other than biking. Let alone what they do for work, where they live, etc."

It all stung, but what lit a wild hair on my ass to do something about it was when Nick singled out one lonely night of the year: the Night Before Thanksgiving. We both remembered how legendary that night had been, the unofficial reunion that went off each year with no planning or explanation, only the name of the bar where we were starting.

I can't remember the last time I went out on the Night Before Thanksgiving. Nick said he felt horrible sitting there each year, unable to think of who he'd even call to grab a beer.

"What happened?" he asked me.

I suppose, in retrospect, I should have taken this particular question as rhetorical.

On the next Night Before Thanksgiving, I sat down at an empty bar in Harvard Square, in a restaurant my buddy owned. I'd worked there a million years before, and he'd given me the entire second floor for the night. The name of the place is Daedalus. He's the dad from Greek mythology who famously advised his son, Icarus, against being cocky and flying too close to the sun. That guy. But I'm not one for signs.

Unlike Senior Skip Day, this reunion didn't require anyone to cut out of work on a Friday, and it was perhaps the one night of the year when most everyone would be in the area and presumably available. It felt so obvious that I didn't even compliment my brain for the idea, and it got off to a good start when the first guest showed up more or less on time.

What followed is tricky to describe, for the guy who walked up the stairs was someone I knew from high school but was not close with, and he was nervous as fuck, which made me nervous as fuck. He told me he wasn't sure he should come, and that he didn't really keep in touch with anyone from high school, or with anyone at all. He said he was hungry and ordered fish and chips, and I sat with him while he ate and he again told me he wasn't sure why he had come.

Rory, my co-host, finally showed up, late as always, and we pounded a quick beer to avoid stating the obvious about this little event. I would say it was a failure, but that would be an insult to failures. This was a festering catastrophe.

No one walked up those stairs. Not a single person. Of all the people who might have come, none did. Just me, Rory, and the guy who didn't know why he had come.

My phone hummed constantly with the usual sorrys and couldn't-sneak-outs and I'm-cooking-this-years and have-a-beer-for-mes. Which was nice, I guess. But no one walked up those stairs. Hours later, after the one guy had left and I was fixing to do the same, an old friend named Chris showed up after a family party. We ordered another round and had a nice laugh at the absolute disaster that was unfolding, but I was ready to tuck my tail between my legs and get out of there.

I had no intention of getting into the business of being the guy who keeps wanting to have high school reunions, but so many people had told me they couldn't make Senior Skip Day and urged me to keep trying. So I doubled down on the idea that people were willing to do slightly more than say "It's been too long." Yet it hadn't worked. As I walked out of the bar alone, a loser again, for real this time, I finally woke up to something I should have known already.

I had to prioritize who to give a fuck about if I was going to figure out how to give a fuck about them.

A few days later, I saw nearly everyone I was hoping to see walk up those stairs that night. All my closest friends from high school. The guys and the girls. The people I would normally be so excited to get together with. But this was not a moment of celebration. It was its opposite.

The younger brother of a popular classmate had died. I knew him pretty well and he was an all-time funny kid, but I had lost touch with him and didn't know he'd been "struggling," as we say in polite company, that sad defining characteristic of an ailment that has made middle-aged white people the only demographic in America whose mortality is on the rise.

I don't know how my friend died, but I do know his death

would fall into that broad category known as "deaths of despair," a term coined by Anne Case and Angus Deaton, husband-and-wife economists at Princeton whose research has revealed that death rates have been steadily rising among middle-aged Americans, particularly white Americans, since 1999, reversing a century-long run in the other direction that brought historic gains.

That cohort—my cohort—is suffering from an onslaught of health crises. An epidemic of depression. Rampant alcoholism. Fatal overdoses, mostly from prescription drugs. A suicide rate that's rising rapidly, especially for men. And the fucking obesity certainly isn't helping. It's a pile of bad news, and the evidence pointed Case and Deaton toward one undeniable conclusion— there was an underlying malaise in America.

Each year, the United Nations puts out its World Happiness Report. For 2017 and 2018, the entire final chapter was devoted to the United States. But not in a good way; instead, they attempted to analyze our slide toward unhappiness, which the report identifies as a full-blown health crisis. Despite our wealth, we ranked just eighteenth in happiness in the 2018 report, down from fourteenth. We currently sit just ahead of the British, but I suspect they will soon gain the upper hand, for the U.K., perhaps more than any other country, has started to systematically combat loneliness as the chief culprit of unhappiness and malaise, particularly with its seniors. The Campaign to End Loneliness has been diligently campaigning on behalf of the issue since 2011, and in 2017 the government created an official cabinet position for a "Minister of Loneliness."

To address the malaise, though, we must address how we're checking off our intrinsic values. According to self-determination theory, human beings require three things to be content: to feel competent at what they do; to feel authentic in their lives; and to feel connected to others.

Loneliness is an ancient feeling, but modernity has brought new dangers to the table. Our tribal ancestors were rarely alone. They saw the same people every single day. They knew everyone, and everyone knew them. If you asked me to point my finger at the absolute zenith of human society, when our species seemed to be handling most of the big questions in the cleanest of ways, I'd zero in on Native American societies just before the northern Europeans invaded along with their poisonous extrinsic values— things like money and class and authority, a culture that prized market and state over community and family. You know, those things that remain our devils.

Attention to the extrinsic has no doubt siphoned our attention away from the intrinsic. And the biggest enemy in that "feel connected to others" category has always been time itself. We evolved a bigger brain, and with it the ability to have an expanded social circle. There's a strong argument for that being the reason we evolved the big brain. But the quality of our connections was and remains directly connected to how much time we actually spend with one another.

I removed some artwork from a wall in my office at home, got a fresh Sharpie and a stack of Post-it notes, and started writing down names. I began by picking through the contacts in my phone, then scrolled through my 1,335 Facebook friends. Many of the choices were easy. My wife. My parents. Grandma. My younger brother in California. The Danimal, my freshman roommate. Two girls I'd first met in fourth grade. My sister-in-law, most days. Six people I'd met through my kids. Twenty-three journalists, which is way too many, including six from grad school. Seven people I grew up with in Southie, which is definitely too many. Eight people I went to high school with, and eight people I went to college with. Five were former roommates. Thirty-five were women. Seven were people I met when I wrote a story about them.

Several of the choices surprised me—people who felt so random, yet I lit up immediately at the sight of their name. More surprising was the ease of the omissions, how quickly I was able to look at the name of a person I knew, often very well, and know I didn't find them very interesting. Still surprising was that I didn't feel like I was doing anything wrong, for I could definitely say I liked nearly all of the people whose names scrolled past my eyes. I'd stop and say hello if I ran into them in a bar. But would I be embarrassed to join them for a drink? That was one of Robin Dunbar's ways of drawing the line at whether you have a meaningful social relationship with another human—a number that was limited, he said, to 150.

Dunbar's number, as it is known, is one of the most discussed theories in social psychology, the work of an Oxford professor who has spent a long career doing research in all corners of social evolution. Everywhere I read, Robin Dunbar's name appeared again and again. I've already referred to a few of his studies. He asks the best questions.

The number 150 was not a theory but a calculation, based on

the size of the neocortex. In studies of primates and other mammals, Dunbar found that the ratio between the volume of the neocortex and the volume of the total brain could accurately predict the size of the animal's social group. When he applied that math to the neocortex of *Homo sapiens*, he came to the number 150.

Dunbar's number came out in the late 1980s during a hot time at Oxford for evolutionary thinking, when young scholars like Richard Dawkins were arguing that our genes are selfish, and that evolution and natural selection are not the stories of an organism but the stories of its DNA competing to live on in future generations, since nearly every bit of heritable information we pass on to the next generation happens in a chemical instant at the moment of conception.

Dunbar proposed what is now known as the social brain hypothesis, which argues that human intelligence evolved primarily as a means of surviving and reproducing in a large group. The patterns of behavior we inherit from our ancestors have been molded by this long game of survival of the fittest just as much as the bodies they're housed in. We're born with rules that guide us.

Dunbar proposed that every person had their own social fingerprint, but in general most people had a group of 150 that broke down thus: Five "very close" friends, plus your romantic partner if you have one. Then you have ten "close" friends, who combine with the "very close" friends to fill out what he called your "sympathy group"—the people who always come to your birthday and cry at your funeral. From there, you have thirty-five people who are in the middle ground between close friends and acquaintances, and then you have about one hundred "acquaintances."

We of course *know* far more people than that. Statistically, we're able to put names to faces for abut fifteen hundred people, Dunbar showed, but constraints in time and bandwidth limit us to right around 150 "friends," he argues.

I'm still not sure if 150 sounds like a lot or a little, but I do know that to keep up with that many required humans to take giant leaps in how we handled social grooming. In nonhuman primates, grooming is done one-on-one through physical touch, which is inefficient. Humans developed music and dance and storytelling and laughter as ways to connect with more than one person at a time, in sync. We can groom many people at once through dancing, as the New Kids on the Block have taught us. But Dunbar found laughter to be exceptionally potent, delivering an endorphin hit three times as effective as physical grooming. (He also found the optimal laughter group size is three people. For a conversation, the number is four.)

Dunbar's great questions came with great answers, but by putting numbers on fluid social actions, he was practically daring people to prove him wrong. Yet decades later, that has not happened; instead, people have continued to find anecdotal evidence of 150 popping up in all sorts of places, from the size of military companies dating back to the Romans to the average number of Christmas cards Brits send out each year. It's easy to see this number if you're looking for it, of course. Many corporations have successfully adopted it as a mantra in their organizational structures. But the best supporting case I've heard comes from the fact that 150 is the average size of a clan in the surviving hunter-gatherer societies.

. . .

I began counting the names on my wall. It looked like a lot, if I'm honest, but as I hit one hundred and looked ahead I got that tingly feeling that Dunbar was about to drain his shot.

One forty-five. One forty-six. One forty-seven. One forty-eight.

I dashed downstairs to go tell my wife about this strange shit I'd been doing with a Sharpie—and also to make sure she didn't call the police, because there aren't too many sane people who cover their walls with Post-it notes that have names written on them. But as soon as the door to my office opened I felt a shooting pang of guilt. For that's when I heard the voices of my children.

In my defense, they have neither phone numbers nor Facebook accounts.

Charlie Baker. One forty-nine.

Jake Baker. One fifty.

Creepy.

When the goose bumps had worn off, I moved the names into groups. The largest grouping was the 23 journalists, which I again assure you is way too many, but I've been working for two decades and that's what happens. Accidents of proximity. That's the term I'd used in my original article to describe work friends, which inspired one of my work friends to declare to me that she was "offended!" I'll admit it's kind of an aggressive statement, but really all friends begin as accidents of proximity. There's a word for those who are not accidents: "family." Friends are the family you choose, and we can only choose from the people who are in proximity.

I stepped back and looked at the names on the wall from afar, then stepped in to again divide the data, this time along a simple, painful line—which of these people do I actively socialize with, and which do I need to work on?

Most needed work, but on the side of what was actually working, two groups stood out. One involved a cult I'd recently joined. More on that later.

The other consisted of two brothers who were half my age.

I'm going to tell you a story.

Back in 2011, two other reporters and I worked together on a long project, a series called "Life on the Line," where we told stories themed around a particular bus route that snaked through some of the rougher neighborhoods in Boston. We worked on the project for months, and as the series moved toward a close, I had it in my head that I wanted to end with an uplifting story. Too often, when it comes to such communities, journalists highlight the struggles and neglect the successes.

I was poking around for a while, unsure of what I was looking for, until I met a social worker named Emmett Folgert, who told me he had my story. Their names were George and Johnny.

Emmett is a tall guy who wears a scally cap and runs a youth center in a cramped space across the street from a McDonald's. The entire thing is held together with spit and bubble gum, but many of the children in the neighborhood are high-risk, and Emmett had been doing incredible work, child by child, for decades.

In the neighborhood, he was famous for carrying dollar bills, which he gave to kids so they could run to McDonald's and get something to eat from the dollar menu, on the condition that they came back and talked to him. He likes to say that you can't talk to a kid if they're hungry.

George and Johnny were two of those hungry kids. They came for the dollars, then stayed around the youth center to play Ping-Pong and video games, gradually opening up to Emmett about what was going on at home. Their parents had emigrated from Vietnam, where their father had fought alongside the U.S. Army. After we choppered out, he spent five years in a communist "reeducation camp." He had lifelong mental health issues, and shortly before I met George and Johnny he had jumped to his death from the tallest bridge in Boston.

Their mother had her own mental health struggles. She didn't speak English. She rarely left the house. She rarely did much of anything. George and Johnny were forced to pretty much raise themselves, and that bus route played a big part in that. It's how they got themselves each day to Boston Latin School.

That's a story I already knew well, as it was that same school that transformed my own life. Boston Latin is the oldest public school in America, and remains one of its best ideas. The top entrance-exam school in the city, it draws kids from all walks of life and then offers them something that's lacking in many neighborhoods: opportunity.

I spent a month going to school with George and Johnny each day, riding the bus, learning their story. George was 14 and painfully shy and quiet; Johnny was a year older, more outgoing but nervous, constantly worried about money and food and their future. As a reporter, my job was to observe, which meant standing silently through problems I could have solved. Once I held my tongue when Johnny didn't have enough money for a movie ticket. They asked me constantly if I could get them free copies of the newspaper when their story ran. I had told them it was going to publish on a Sunday, and they had figured out that the Sunday paper cost a lot more than the other days.

The night before their story ran, I picked them up and took them to the *Globe*'s printing plant so they could pull their story straight off the line. We went for pizza afterward, and suddenly our relationship felt different. The wall was gone. I was no longer a reporter. I was their friend, and that friendship came to mean so much in all our lives.

At first, I was the adult who filled in the cracks. Rides. Prom tickets. Christmas gifts. That sort of thing. Emmett coached me on being a mentor, taught me to stay on them, to ask questions, to step in when I had guidance to give. They did their part the way they always had—by keeping their heads down, staying out of trouble, and excelling in school. Johnny got a scholarship to UMass Amherst to study chemical engineering. I drove him to his first day of school, bought him a dorm fridge, and teared up when it was time to leave him on his own.

The next year, I was sitting in the newsroom one afternoon when George texted me: "I got in!" He had been accepted to Yale. I got so emotional that I retreated to the cafeteria, and before I had really thought it through I started writing a confessional story, line by line on Twitter, of all places, about how much our relationship meant to me. Those tweets went viral, and all of a sudden we were being held up as some shining example of whatever people wanted us to be. *NBC Nightly News* immediately sent a star reporter up from New York in a blizzard. CNN flew us to Los Angeles. Seemingly every major website had something to say about us, and I was frankly getting way too much credit for Johnny's and George's accomplishments. It felt very momentous, but the truth was that our relationship succeeded because it was light. Emmett was their father figure; I got to play the part of the fun uncle. I didn't wake them up and get them on that bus and do their homework. The best thing I had done for them was really so simple. I had become their phone call.

Beginning in 1938, researchers at Harvard University began tracking 724 sophomores for a longitudinal health study. Formally known as the Harvard Study of Adult Development, it has become better known as the "Harvard Happiness Study." That's because it has produced the best long-term data on the connection between health and happiness, and how we actually get there.

From the very beginning, the researchers have been asking the subjects a simple question that has incredibly telling results: Who would you call in the middle of the night if you were sick or afraid?

Those who had someone to turn to in that moment were statistically healthier and happier. They also aged better and lived longer than people who lacked warm, close relationships.

I've been through a lot with George and Johnny. Births and birthdays. Terrifying driving lessons. Thanksgivings at my parents' house. First girlfriends and first heartbreaks. Graduations and first jobs. They've become like family. They even call me Uncle Billy, though that's typically when they're busting my balls for being old, which they do constantly.

They've grown up before my eyes, and as they dipped their toes into adulthood they gradually stopped needing me as much as they once did. Three or four times a year they'll come spend the weekend with my family, and it's amazing to see how much they've grown and blossomed out of their shells, seeming as comfortable as people can be in those messy years of their early twenties. I can't take credit for any of it, except for perhaps that one simple thing. I have been their phone call. And they know I always will be.

Now to the other group on my Post-it wall. This one is a bit embarrassing, if I'm being honest. I never wanted to be the middle-aged guy who had "friends from the gym." Health clubs hold zero appeal for me. They always felt like a weird world of silent competition, a social space that seemed to follow the unwritten decorum of the urinal—eyes forward, no talking, just do your business and go. Everyone wearing headphones, communicating in ape-like gestures to ask if you're done with that bench.

I was always a team sports guy. I loved being a part of the herd, of talking it up on the bench and ball busting in the locker room. I'm the sort who bit into the romance of "playing for the guy next to you." But that stuff ends too quickly, and all of a sudden you're supposed to get your exercise by exercising, and no thanks.

Unfortunately, the dad bod comes for everyone, and something must be done about it. Continuing with the clichés, I became a runner, pounding the pavement for long distances alone with my headphones, which is as horrible as it sounds. I have never loved running. I loved the feeling of having run. I loved watching my gut shrink. But I never loved running, especially alone. I knew I needed something else. And I still can't believe what that something was.

Let me head you off right here and point out that prior to actually joining a CrossFit gym, I was probably the world's leader in making jokes about people who did CrossFit. At the very least, I was in the top ten. And that was mostly because of the issue that's addressed in the greatest CrossFit joke of all: "How do you know someone does CrossFit? Because they'll tell you."

The person to blame for all of this was my college buddy Matt. He was my partner in my first marathon, and he practically dragged me through the final miles. This happened despite the fact that I had run way more training miles than he had. Instead of running, that asshole had done CrossFit. Even worse, he made it sound like much more fun than running.

The way he explained it is that he'd go to his gym, where he had made a couple of buddies, and they would have a couple of laughs and do a warm-up and then a short workout—very often with a partner or a small team—and then be out the door in an hour, all happy and shit from the endorphins. It sounds awful, amiright?

We had another marathon coming up, in the fall, and I had no desire to log miles alone in the hot summer sun, so I signed up for a three-month membership at CrossFit Cape Ann, promising myself that I was just going to get a little stronger and then get the hell out of there when the weather cooled. Whatever happened, I would never become one of those awful "gym" people.

I loved it right away. There, I said it. And it gets worse. What I liked the most was the social aspect. Everything is done in classes, grinding though things in a group, encouraging and complaining together, shoulder to shoulder. It's an elective hardship, just like marathoning, which is weird if you think about it, but we live in a world where most people's day-to-day lives are missing the physical work our bodies were made for. But there's no use lamenting what got us here; instead, it was wonderful to simply accept the primitive benefits that come from going through a challenge with another human being. And since many workouts are designed so that a partner is depending on you—for example, they can't stop doing sit-ups until you finish rowing four hundred meters—you feel genuinely necessary to them. And feeling necessary to one another during a time of struggle is the ancient recipe for tribe formation. It's why people often report, in retrospect, that they were happiest during times of war or disaster. Those are times you feel necessary to your neighbor; when it's over you go back inside your house and lock the door and sue your neighbor if their fence comes a foot over your property line.

Another loser fact about joining a community-based gym: the pre- and post-workout chatting was the most socializing I did each day. Again, I could wallow in navel-gazing about how sad that is, or I could appreciate the fact it had become such a positive in my life that when I sat down and made a list of the 150 people I gave a shit about in this world, 11 of them were gym friends. They were the people I saw most often in a social setting, during the hour each day when I consistently had the most fun, when the endorphins had me in the best mood, so it makes total sense, even though saying it out loud still feels weirdly embarrassing.

One of the people I became closest to through the gym was a guy named Andrew. We had met at our kids' preschool, and he was a journalist as well, and we hit it off right away and had a beer here and there, but that seemed to be about all it was going to be. Then one day I happened to be near his office, so I stopped in to say hello. "We need to grab a beer," he said as I was leaving. To which I countered, soooo awkwardly, "This is going to sound crazy, but instead of that, would you want to come to my gym with me sometime?" He made the obligatory eye rolls when I said the word "CrossFit," but he showed up one Saturday morning, and the next thing I knew he was guzzling the Kool-Aid.

Just like that, we started to see each other most mornings, which meant we quickly went from two guys who liked each other and kept saying they wanted to hang out to actual full-blown bros. This of course meant that every woman who knew us—in particular his teenage daughter—was falling over herself to label our relationship a "bromance." That's a term that was coined in the nineties by the skateboarding magazine *Big Brother* to describe skaters who spent a ton of time together, but it has morphed into a gentle insult for any guys who dare get too close. It's not as condescending as "bros," and it doesn't cut quite as wrong as being shouted down with "gaaay." No, the bromance lived in the category of the oh-aren't-you-cute pat on the head.

What's saddest to me is that the reason we even need a term for bromance is because it's so rare it must be pointed at. But openly close male friendships are enough of an anomaly in this day and age that you need something to call it.

I'm gonna tell you something else that's rare: spending two hundred hours interacting with a new friend. That's the point at which, according to a 2018 study in the *Journal of Social and Personal Relationships*, people are able to cross the line into good/best friends. Outside of work, the only place that could possibly happen for me is at the gym. The difference is that work interactions—like a huge chunk of interactions in our daily life—have an economic basis. Even if it's just in the tiniest of ways, money is an undercurrent in nearly every encounter we have. Think about it. To succeed in business, you don't make friends; you network. For modern man, the earning or spending of money is the chief reason we need humans outside of our family.

Many scientists remain conflicted about why, then, we even need friends. Technically, you can survive without them. Many people do. More attempt it each day. But the theory that comes up most often to support popularity concerns the ability to assemble a squad when shit hits the fan.

The concept of having a friend's back, and knowing they have yours, is a sacred pact. It's the knowledge that in times of danger and crisis you are not alone. What makes it so special is that it doesn't apply to every friend in the exact same way. There are only so many people you'd jump into a fight for.

I knew exactly who those people were because I'd written their names on 150 Post-it notes like a psychopath. But by defining who was worth fighting for, I had done something equally worthwhile: I had identified who was not. Letting go of problem relationships can be just as important for health and happiness, because they can literally infect you with their bullshit.

Since 1948, researchers have been tracking five thousand people—and now their offspring—from Framingham, Massachusetts, in one of the most important longitudinal studies of health. Perhaps the most groundbreaking finding of that study is that it shows that it's not just germs that are contagious. There are measurable social contagions. Obesity is contagious among social networks, as is smoking.

You can probably see those pretty easily. But perhaps more surprising is that researchers discovered that things like loneliness are contagious. Having a lonely friend makes you statistically more likely to be lonely.

But here's the best part. Happiness is contagious in the exact same way.

So writing those names on my wall was as much about knowing who I cared about as it was about letting go of those whose bullshit was infecting my life.

Once you know who to give a shit about, you can turn your attention to how to give a shit about them.

Seven

*L*ater on in this chapter, there's going to come a moment when I'm seated next to a Yale "happiness professor" in a stately drawing room, and I'm going to nod when she tells me that psychology has the answers to happiness, that you can achieve wellness by being intentional about your social actions.

But to get there, I need to begin a few months earlier, with something that worked specifically because it was unintentional, triggered not by methodology but by spark. Serendipity, with a sprinkling of midlife crisis.

I'm referring to the fact that Rory and I, suddenly and independently, became surfers.

This was a rather curious development, considering that we were 40-something men who lived in a part of the world where the ocean is usually cold enough to kill you. Stranger still was that it was the perfect vehicle for us to give a shit about each other.

It started when I took a lesson with some friends at a beach near my home, stood up on a knee-high wave, felt the energy of the ocean take over, and knew immediately what those asshole surfers had been going on and on about. At the risk of sounding lame, it was a before-and-after experience for me. I knew instantly that I was going to spend a lot of my time trying to chase the sensation I had just experienced.

Amazingly, Rory had had a parallel experience on a trip to Mexico with some college friends. All of a sudden, we were completely smitten with an activity that was so perfectly suited for us that you couldn't possibly arrive at it by decision. This one came from the gods of friendship, because it turns out that surfing is a misleading name, implying as it does that the main activity of a surfer is surfing. To be more clear, let me point at fishing and hunting as being correctly named. They are not called catching and killing.

But surfing is very rarely about surfing. You can't just go do it when you feel like it, particularly in a wave-poor region like Massachusetts. No, you can only surf when the ocean allows it, and those are narrow windows that require constant monitoring of swells and winds and tides so that you might possibly put your neoprene-covered body into the vicinity of a surfable wave. Even then, when your body is actually in the ocean, the chief activity is paddling. And more paddling. And still more paddling, punctuated only, in our case, by dramatic wipeouts when we dared to try to stand up on our boards. It was an activity that required constant tending and vigorous effort. In other words, it required a hunting buddy with the same narrow addiction.

Surfing kept us in constant contact, trying to figure out the million things there were to figure out. One thing we did decode, early on, was that surfing is not really a summer activity. That's only in the movies. No, surfing is a winter sport, for that's when the storms churn up the ocean; it's just that winters in Hawaii look a tad different than winters in New England.

So when the waves would come on those frozen mornings, we would dash off at dawn with our boards strapped to the roof of my aging station wagon, usually to the New Hampshire seacoast, which is just 18 miles long but has a road running along most of it, which allowed us to scout various breaks, babbling giddy excitement and fear, as we pretended to know what we were looking for. Nervously, we'd commit to a spot, suit up, rush to the shoreline, stare at the icy ocean with crippling fear, and then paddle out together, each enabled by the knowledge that someone had his back in that big freezing ocean.

When we could stand the cold no longer, we'd rush out of the ocean, shivering, and speed through what became a well-choreographed routine of yanking the other person's wet suit off their shoulders as fast as possible so we could get in the car and blast the heater. Always, it would feel like we'd gone through something together, which is the ancient fermentation process for brewing friendship.

Seeing as we were surfer bros and all, Rory and I decided we needed to go on a surf trip to one of those places where winter looks very different. We chose the Nicoya Peninsula in Costa Rica, which is known to surfers for its consistent waves and warm water, and to scientists for being one of the world's Blue Zones.

We were about an hour south of Liberia, the capital city of

Guanacaste Province, bouncing along potholed dirt roads in our tiny rental car, when we entered this so-called Blue Zone. I felt my senses heighten, as every face that appeared outside our windows, every home that we passed, could hold some clue, some lesson toward the goal of trying to figure out what they were doing that I was not.

"The Blue Zones" is a term that was first popularized by Dan Buettner in a 2005 article in *National Geographic* magazine, in which he identified five hot spots in the world where people live measurably longer, happier, and healthier lives, with a fraction of the diseases of the developed world. It should not surprise you to learn that much of their success is attributed to strong social connections. (They also eat a lot of legumes.)

The five Blue Zones consisted of the inner mountains of Sardinia, an island in the Mediterranean, where it's not uncommon for men to live to see 100; Okinawa, Japan, where quality of life is celebrated and long health spans are the outcome; Loma Linda, California, where a community of Seventh-day Adventists reap the benefits of clean living to the tune of ten more years of life than the typical North American; and the Greek island of Icaria, where a third of people live to their nineties and dementia is virtually nonexistent.

And then there was the Blue Zone I was now driving through, which felt like it had something particular to teach me. I'd awoken that morning at home, in a country where being middle-aged was increasingly deadly. Now a plane ride and a rental car had put my coordinates dead-center in the spot with the lowest middle-age mortality on earth.

Buettner identified specific lifestyle traits that run through each of the Blue Zones, including constant moderate physical activity (think gardening rather than marathoning or CrossFit); intentional routines to deal with stress (the Greeks nap, and the Sardinians hit happy hour); and plant-based diets with moderate caloric intake (amazingly, people in all five zones eat a light dinner in the early evening—the smallest meal of the day—and then nothing else). The zones also shared some sort of engagement in religion, or at the very least spirituality. And with the exception of the Adventists, they all drink in moderation, typically a glass or two of wine per day. There is also the idea of a purpose in life, a reason to wake up in the morning. The Nicoyans refer to this as *"plan de vida,"* and simply knowing your reason can add years to your life.

But what most interested me, and what had my eyes overanalyzing every local man and woman we came across in Nicoya—*ticos* and *ticas*, as they are known—was the entire corner of the Blue Zone theory that attributed so much of this wellness to strong social connections with friends and family. All the zones practiced the original form of social security, which meant keeping elderly parents and grandparents in close proximity, often in the same home.

And so it was that I approached my week in Nicoya with a specific filter on my brain. This is a dangerous mindset—that of the strolling anthropologist—for it is quite easy to find consequence in the inconsequential. This is especially perilous if you're a sun-soaked, vacation-brained, surfed-out gringo in a tropical paradise.

So I will throttle back the many, many notes I made, most of them the intellectual equivalent of buying a puka shell necklace, and serve you the one that felt most concrete, and the one I was most jealous of. And like every darn epiphany on this journey, it was so damn simple.

I'm referring to the obvious fact that in the afternoons and evenings, when the heat finally let go and there was shade to be had, everyone congregated in groups outdoors. Kids and dogs, grandpas and neighbors, everyone hanging out, often around an open fire and the smell of something cooking, the most primitive and satisfying of ways for humans to end a day.

I thought of my own social circles, where such gatherings are so few and far between that they were deemed "special occasions." This felt sad.

Even sadder was that by American standards, it felt normal.

Now let me get back to the Yale happiness professor selling me, with the conviction of a street-corner preacher, the idea that psychology has the answers.

I had arrived in New Haven the previous day, having made the two-hour drive down from Boston to see this woman, and also to see for myself why what she was selling was so popular on campus. I had come a day early because George wanted me to do something that was utterly preposterous: He wanted me to spend the night in his dorm and hang out with his friends.

I'd been to Yale many times with George, having driven him there or picked him up, though I'd never spent much time actually hanging out. We'd usually hit Frank Pepe's, New Haven's legendary pizza place, and then get back on the road. But it was the spring of George's senior year, and I knew he really wanted me to meet his friends and see what his life was like at Yale, so I committed to spend the night in a tiny dorm bed for the first time in two decades.

As George led me on a tour through his college life, from the stately residence hall though the stately quad to the stately dining hall, I could feel my inner old-man voice grumbling, "Fuck Yale." This statement works for every college and college student, and it is muttered with seething old-man jealousy. But it feels especially apt for the fancy old schools like Yale, which have become so good at the things that are so great about college—those things that don't really exist anywhere else in life and make the undergrad experience, in the words of the Yale fight song, "the shortest, gladdest years of life."

Yale, in particular, does something that is rather ingenious socially, which is that it splits its six thousand undergraduates into 14 residential colleges, that each look and feel an awful lot like the houses at Hogwarts in the Harry Potter books. Each house contains a few hundred students—a much more manageable network size—and is headed by a faculty member who actually lives there, usually with a family in tow, and provides the stabilizing presence of having a parent in the house. The social center of each residential college is its dining hall. They each have their own, and they are not the cafeterias of my youth. No, the dining hall for Timothy Dwight College, where George lived, was so damn reminiscent of the dining hall at Hogwarts that I'm just going to keep saying

"Harry Potter." It was the first place George wanted to drag me once I'd dropped my bags.

It was unusually tough for me to be curmudgeonly as George and I walked through the Yale campus, for I was just so damn proud of the young man he'd become. I don't think he said five words during the first five days I spent shadowing him to high school; now this painfully shy kid was stopping constantly to introduce me to each person we passed, offering up a quick glowing biography for each of them, with the people skills of a politician. It was very obvious that George loved Yale. Loved it. Which is why I could sense the sadness and uncertainty and humming anxiety of knowing that someday soon it would all end. With the rug just a month away from being pulled out from under him, anticipatory nostalgia had given way to a palpable panic. Not only would the end of college take with it this huge, active, stable social network he had built, but it would also bring to an end the only predictable path that he, and his classmates, had been promised—just do your homework and get good grades and you will achieve.

For George and the rest of them, getting into Yale had been their crowning achievement. Every student I met was clearly a hardworking, type A, annoyingly accomplished SuperKid. Now they were looking at the real world rushing toward them and being forced to consider where to put all that striving when achievement was no longer so easily measurable.

On the topic of the future, George was an absolute mess; every time I spoke to him he had a new plan. And if you want to see a SuperKid achiever type in a panic, catch them in a mood when they feel like they're falling behind their classmates. On a campus full of overachievers, such feelings come at you constantly.

As an adult who has survived all this and come out the other side, I find that watching young people put this much pressure on themselves inspires a particular feeling.

Laurie Santos, the professor I'd come to see, would describe that adult feeling to me in very simple terms when we met the following morning. She was explaining what had motivated her to create the class that immediately became the most popular in the three-hundred-plus-year history of Yale University, and she described it as a desire to scream two simple words at the students.

"Chill out."

I met Santos in the drawing room of Silliman College, where she lived with her husband. They had moved in two years before when she became the head of the college, and she quickly found herself assuming the role of den mother to nearly five hundred students. This is when she first developed that desire to scream.

Santos is a psychology professor, but her specialty was in how nonhuman primates interact. But undergrads proved to be an entirely different animal, and she told me that she was blown away by the amount of pressure they had put on themselves, which wrecked their stress levels and their sleep and their mental health, which combined to take away their happiness.

Santos is my age but could pass for an undergrad. She has long ringlets of dark brown hair, and the kind of soft, friendly face that invites people to let their guard down and begin confession. At least that's how it worked with me, as I spent too much of our time ranting about how stressed it made me to see George and his friends so stressed.

She herself had gone to Harvard as an undergrad, so she was not naïve to the pressures of being a student at such a place. But she felt that the problem had become much worse, and societal cues backed her up, with the skyrocketing rates of anxiety and depression and suicide all around. "We've been on a path as a society that is not great and must come to an end," she declared.

And that is when she turned to me and, in a practiced, soothing voice, told me what I'd come to hear.

"The psychology research has the answers to happiness."

She told me that as she began diving into the research and planning the course, she did so based around the idea that we have a fundamental misconception about what makes us happy. We chase it through external circumstances, the idea that if we only got a better grade, or made more money, or had a nicer home, and on and on.

To counter that, she brought together work on positive psychology and behavior change, then put them into applied form to create a class where "the goal was to rewire the way students viewed the pursuit of happiness. And we know from psychology that the top key to happiness has to do with intentional social interactions. Very happy people spend time with other people."

Let me pause here and point out how weird it was to hear all this, for Laurie Santos had no clue about me and the journey I was on. Yes, I had mentioned my concerns about the stress George was under, but other than that I was just another reporter doing an interview, one she had now done a couple of times, for the course had turned Santos into something of a media darling. I bring this up now to give myself a pat on the back for maintaining my professional composure and not interjecting constantly to yell "Preach!"

Psyc 157, Psychology and the Good Life, became a phenomenon the moment it was announced. Some twelve hundred students enrolled in the course when it was unveiled that semester. That's nearly a quarter of Yale's undergrads. One of those students was George.

Enrollment in the happiness class, as everyone came to call it, was so unprecedented that the meeting space had to be moved to Woolsey Hall, a cathedral-like auditorium typically used for things like symphony concerts. To handle the volume of students, Santos had to employ two dozen teaching fellows.

To capitalize on the popularity, Yale had quickly begun producing an online version called The Science of Well-Being. When I spoke with Santos, it had been out for just a month but had already been taken by seventy-eight thousand people in 168 countries.

At this point, I can't say any of this surprised me. Just a few weeks before my trip to Yale, I'd flown to Austin, Texas, to appear on a panel about loneliness and happiness at South by Southwest. As I walked through the convention hall to the room where my panel was being held, I saw a long line snaking down the hallway, and being naturally nosy I inquired who everyone was waiting for. The festival schedule was packed with big-name speakers. I nearly had a heart attack when I found out they were waiting for my panel, which had sold out so quickly that organizers scheduled a second one for later the same day.

In the case of Laurie Santos, what she was selling clearly had buyers. But what exactly *was* she selling?

A few hours after sitting with Santos, I walked with George and some of his friends to attend Psychology and the Good Life. Woolsey Hall is an incredible space, and after first sitting with his crew on the ground level I decided I wanted a more sweeping view and moved up to the circular balcony that ringed the auditorium, hoping to see how this mass colony of students reacted to her sermon.

But as the class began, I could see an immediate flaw in my plan. And that was because there was hardly anyone there.

As Santos prowled the grand stage, wearing a wireless microphone and pacing back and forth in front of a huge screen, the whole thing felt more TED Talk than college class. The lecture, number 18 of the course, focused on being "slaves to our habits," and stressed the idea of using positive cues as a way to "hack" those habits. Her presentation straddled the line between a traditional psychology class, with deep dives into the research, and a self-help seminar, which included Santos's "psych pro tips" and "rewirement requirements," which were actual assignments for breaking those bad habits and creating new ones.

But where were all the students? I counted about two hundred people, which meant a full one thousand students had cut the class. The room was so empty as to feel awkward.

I have two theories. The first, and most optimistic, is that the students had, in fact, taken Santos up on her advice. As she had told me, and George had enthusiastically backed up, her most popular assignment had come earlier in the semester, on the topic of "time affluence."

To deliver this lecture, she waited until all the students were gathered in their seats, and then she informed them that there would be no class. Instead, she ordered them to use the unexpected free time creatively, with some rules. No schoolwork and no phones. The goal was for them to get up from their seats and go do something, preferably together.

The typical Yale student lives in a state of perpetual "time famine," so this news was received dramatically. Santos told me that two students in front of her immediately burst out in tears. The way George relayed it to me—this gift of a couple fucking hours of free time—it was like he'd found water in the desert.

The students went off in groups and did all sorts of crazy things and nothing at all. More than a few reported they went back to their dorms and took a glorious nap. Then the experiment got an unexpected extension when Yale announced they were canceling school for the following day because a huge snowstorm was arriving. New friendships were made. New places were explored. Snowmen were built. Many of the students stayed together all through the night.

So as I sat up in the balcony doing a finger count of the students, it was possible that those thousand missing students were practicing time affluence, and potentially working on their final project, which was to implement something non–school related—like meditation, or exercise, or even friggin' sleep—into their lives.

That was my optimistic take on why the joint was a ghost town. Option two, and the one I feared was more likely, was that "happiness" had become a blowoff class. And this being Yale and all, I suspected students were not using their time affluence for self-care but were instead stressing over all the shit that made them enroll in a happiness class in the first place.

When the lecture was over, I went to lunch with George and some of the other students, and their review of the course was very lukewarm. They liked it but didn't love it, and there was a feeling that they'd gotten the gist of it early on. The lessons had value, they agreed, but they seemed to shelve them as the sort of things that are "good to know."

The students certainly didn't think the lessons would help with landing a good job or getting into a good grad school. You know, the important things.

A few weeks after my visit to Yale, my twenty-fifth high school re-union rolled around, followed two days later by my birthday. The confluence of these two events brought to a head something that had been percolating since SXSW and had come up in interesting ways during my trip to New Haven. Yet it was that one-two punch of a reunion and a birthday that forced me to finally take a position on something many people had asked me about. And that was the role of social media in friendship and loneliness.

It was a topic I had avoided in my original article, and then kind of sidestepped ever since, usually pointing out that I'd yet to see any conclusive evidence of its effect on loneliness. There were studies that showed those who felt lonely or socially isolated spent more time online than those who did not. A 2017 study in the *American Journal of Preventive Medicine* found that young adults who used social media the most, defined as more than 50 visits a week, tripled the odds that they would feel socially isolated over those who went online nine times or less. But there was a chicken-and-egg problem in such research. It was unclear whether social media made people feel lonely, which would mean it was bad, or if the already lonely went to social media looking for connection, in which case I'd argue it was good.

It was a question I fielded several times in interviews and on panels, and I'd always slide out the side door by pointing out that the evidence didn't feel solid in either direction, so it was up to each person to decide whether it felt healthy for them. Which is just a roundabout way of saying I was struggling to figure out whether it was healthy for me.

When I was in the Yale dorm that night, George made some sort of crack about my being old, and I responded by saying, "Tell me about it; I've got my twenty-fifth high school reunion in a couple weeks." One of George's friends had stopped by, and he chimed in to say that he had a theory that Facebook had largely rendered reunions unnecessary, for it had robbed everyone of the joy of catching up. Several light bulbs lit up in my brain, and there was much to unpack, but the conversation moved elsewhere and I gave it no more thought. Then the following day, when I was having my conversation with Laurie Santos, she mentioned an accidental breakthrough that some of her students had had. During a lecture, she had mentioned a study that showed people who quit social media reported being happier, and a few of her eager-beaver students misinterpreted that as an assignment to quit social media. And sure as shit, when they reported the results of their accidental assignment, it was with the same outcome: They felt happier.

My own personal experience with social media feels fairly typical. If I were to chart my emotions over time, it would show an early spike—"I've reconnected with so many friends! This is the best thing ever!"—and then a slow and steady decline toward "This is the dumpster fire that's going to swallow society!" There were many reasons for the shift in my affections, but much of it was personal disappointment for allowing myself to become conditioned to checking social media seemingly every time I touched my phone. It was the Pavlovian version of opening the fridge when you're bored rather than hungry. Yet for all of social media's evils, there was no denying that it always came with that quick-hit feeling that I was no longer alone each time my screen lit up.

Then my twenty-fifth reunion arrived and I can't say I gave it much thought. I wasn't nervous, or anxious, or much of anything. I looked forward to seeing my friends, sure. Mark and Rory would be there, as would a few others who were still in my 150. But even for them, who I certainly didn't see enough, the reunion felt like it was a staged event to catch up on stuff that didn't need catching up. I saw them on Facebook. I knew where they worked and what their children's names were. But I also knew roughly the same level of detail for many classmates who were far outside that 150, including some I hadn't seen with my own eyes since we'd finished twelfth grade. It made basic small talk feel unnecessary but deeper conversations still far off, especially in that environment, so I basically said, "Great to see you, you look great," about two hundred times and called it a night.

The next morning, I found myself feeling disappointed that more hadn't come of the opportunity. Was it me? Was it them? Was it all of us? It was the day before my birthday, which meant I was 24 hours from receiving all of those personally impersonal "Hope you have a great day" messages on Facebook. So when I opened up Facebook that morning and saw that ridiculous question "What's on your mind, Billy?" I had a ridiculous answer.

"As Facebook will soon inform you, tomorrow is my birthday," I wrote. "In lieu of writing a message on my wall, I'd love it if you called me. Yes, you. It's been too long."

The following day, nearly 50 people took me up on my request, which was incredibly touching. It took me weeks to call them all back.

Another 134 people wrote "Hope you have a great day" on my wall. I never bothered to write back. Instead, I disabled my Facebook page.

Within a week, I had cleaned everything out of my Twitter account (which I'm technically required to keep for my job). I would have done the same with my Instagram account, but it was already empty because I'd yet to succumb to that addiction. Then I took a step back and admired my phone, which now looked a whole lot more like a tool for productivity rather than a tool for distraction.

I had no idea if what I'd done would make me happy or sad, or if it would make me feel more connected or less. Yes, I knew that studies showed people reported a spike in overall happiness after quitting social media, but knowing is not half the battle. Laurie Santos calls this "The G.I. Joe Fallacy," and it's the best thing I took from my time with her.

If you're of a certain age, you may remember that G.I. Joe cartoons always ended with a character delivering some moral lesson, which always concluded with the statement: "And now you know, and knowing is half the battle." I had never given this statement much thought until I was sitting with Santos and she called bullshit.

"Knowing is *not* half the battle," she semi-shouted at me. "You have to set up better situations. You don't get it for free by knowing something."

This hit me particularly hard because I think I was guilty of believing that knowing was a major accomplishment. In almost everything I'd attempted or observed on my quixotic friendship quest, I at least walked away feeling like I knew something I hadn't known before. I had tried to set up some situations, but many of the big ones were one-offs, stunts; they weren't major changes based on what I knew.

So as much as it scared me to cut myself off from my online circle, I trusted what I knew and made the jump. If I wanted happier-ness, I wouldn't get it for free.

Being shut off from my virtual social group immediately amplified two primal, neglected emotions in me. First, I was reintroduced to feeling bored. It was sad to discover how much of my day had become devoted to dumb-thumbing my way down social media threads. With that gone, and all kinds of new free time in its place, I reconnected with the improvisational world of boredom and found myself doing strange things like staring out the window and thinking.

The second big emotional impact of quitting social media was that it made me miss my friends. I know the easy knock on social media is that it's just people telling you what they had for dinner, but it could be so much more than that. Long before, I had eliminated much of the noise on my feeds, so the friends I "saw" each day were those who made me laugh and learn and think. That was not something I was prepared to lose forever, so it forced me into an interesting position. The only way to get those people back into my life was to actually get them back into my life.

Eight

I stood at the mirror in a crowded men's room at O'Hare International Airport in Chicago and adjusted the wig I'd just pulled from my carry-on. I then continued putting on my disguise, as suspicious onlookers gave me the side-eye and considered whether to call security.

When everything was in place—gray sweatshirt under a denim jacket atop denim jeans, all of it now under a billowing yellow raincoat—I hung a skull-shaped key on a leather string around my neck and gave the ensemble an admiring look in the mirror.

In my head, I had imagined this moment to be more glorious than it was. This is obviously a recurring problem for me. Instead of looking like Mikey from *The Goonies*, the greatest children's movie of my generation, I looked like a guy wearing a Canadian tuxedo with a terrible wig and a raincoat that was apparently sized for André the Giant. But once you commit to an absurd notion, there's no sense in turning back; that would be absurd.

I walked quickly through the crowds at O'Hare with that unmistakable gait that announces "there's nothing to see here"—a doomed gesture that exposes itself in the attempt—as I went in search of my flight to Salt Lake City. I expected my buddy Matt to be waiting at the terminal for me, and I sure as hell expected him to be dressed as Brand, Mikey's older brother.

I hadn't seen Matt in two years, ever since I said good-bye to him and two of my toenails after the Chicago Marathon. He lives outside Chicago, in the suburb that is the setting for John Hughes movies. I may have sprung a small eighties boner when Matt showed me the water tower that was once painted with the words "Save Ferris."

I had arranged to connect at O'Hare so that Matt and I could fly together to Utah to meet the other boys, who were at that moment somewhere in the air over the continental United States, wondering why they had listened to me when I claimed I'd found a single activity that would allow me to take action on basically everything I'd learned about the keys to male friendship, a bonding adventure so perfect in every way that it was as if it had been engineered by social psychologists.

I arrived at the terminal before Matt and tried to blend into the scenery as I did my best to keep my billowing raincoat from accidentally suffocating a small child. Eventually, I spotted Matt sauntering toward me down a long corridor—he's from Oklahoma, and simply refuses to walk faster than cowboy-boot speed, regardless of his footwear—and in the interminable wait it became clear that the only costume he was wearing was that of the suburban dad who works in tech. I believe there was a fleece vest involved.

"You look ridiculous," he said as he hugged me and forty-two hundred square feet of raincoat.

"Where's your costume? We're going on a treasure hunt. We need to be dressed as the Goonies," I interrogated him.

"It's in my bag. I didn't know we were wearing them on the plane."

"When did you think we were wearing them? I'm not going into the wilderness in this crap."

Matt promised to put on his Brand costume when we landed in Salt Lake City, and was forgiven for his grave oversight when, upon boarding the plane, he informed me that he had downloaded *The Goonies* for us to watch on the flight. Which we did, guffawing every time the character Chunk opened his mouth.

When the Rocky Mountains, our ultimate destination, appeared outside the plane windows, I pulled out my earbud and informed Matt for, like, the ninety-eighth time: "We're going to find this treasure."

And in that moment, I genuinely believed it.

Matt leaned over me to look out the window.

"I just hope you don't get us killed," he said.

What am I going on about? I'm glad you asked, because I'm clearly excited to tell you, but first let me acknowledge, and perhaps apologize for, my enthusiasm. It's my personality type, according to my aunt Maria, and something called an enneagram. I don't know if I'd ever heard of an enneagram before, but my aunt Maria declared to me one day that I was "a seven," and that she'd always known I was a seven. She waited until just after my forty-second birthday to announce this fact, which she did after I showed up at a family party with my new skateboard. Rory and I had decided to buy ourselves skateboards for our birthdays, with the goal that if we somehow learned to turn a skateboard, we might translate that into turning a surfboard.

And while buying a skateboard for your forty-second and forty-third birthdays, respectively, when you have never skate-boarded a day in your life may sound like a bad idea, I'm here to assure you that it most definitely is. Eating shit on concrete is not something that goes well with gray hair. But the family party took place at my cousin's house, which is on a quiet street with a slight slope, so I packed the skateboard in the car and snuck out of the party when no one was watching. My aunt Maria caught sight of me through the window and was soon standing on the steps, yell-ing something about the number seven.

When I read up on the enneagram—a type of personality test—and read through the description for number seven, the En-thusiast, I felt like someone had been spying on me. For it defined in clear terms every symptom of my life. I didn't bother taking the test. I'm a seven, and there's no sense in apologizing for things you can't change. Plus, being able to call myself an "enthusiast" was a more elegant way of explaining what my mother has long referred to as my "unicycle problem." This phrase was born out of an oft-told story from my childhood about how I *just had to have* a unicycle but never learned to ride it because I was distracted by whatever enthusiasm came after it. Which is just as well, because riding a unicycle as a child is a strong predictor of having a pony-tail as an adult.

But my enthusiasm for the adventure I was dragging Matt and two other college buddies on is not something that needs an apology. No, I'm pretty sure this one should win me a Nobel Prize of some sort, because this caper so perfectly fit everything I'd learned about male friendship and bonding that it felt engineered for the purpose. And in a way, it was.

In 1988, a wealthy antiques dealer and collector from New Mexico by the name of Forrest Fenn was diagnosed with cancer that was thought to be terminal, and came up with a plan to walk into the Rocky Mountains carrying his greatest treasures. Part two of his plan was to lie down and die. Whoever found his body would get to keep the loot.

This scheme fell apart, much to his surprise, when he beat cancer. Yet the idea never left him, and so, 22 years later, when he was 80, he marched into his beloved Rockies and hid a chest filled with several million dollars' worth of gold coins and trinkets. To find the treasure, all one had to do was figure out a cryptic poem, which he published in his autobiography. As if having to read a poem wasn't bad enough, his clues involved wonderfully vague statements such as "Begin it where warm waters halt" and "There'll be no paddle up your creek."

Since that stupid poem was published, it's estimated that more than one hundred thousand people, probably English majors, have convinced themselves that they'd deciphered the poem and gone looking for Fenn's treasure in the imposing mountains of Montana, Wyoming, Colorado, and New Mexico. Hundreds have quit their jobs to do it full-time. Five have died searching for the treasure (I stressed to my friends that these deaths were classic backcountry fatalities, as if that somehow made them more palatable). Yet it remained undiscovered, at least at the moment we went searching for it. Fenn would later announce that it had been found by some guy from "back east," though he refused to say where exactly the treasure had been hidden, only furthering the suspicion of many that the entire thing is a hoax.

The treasure-hunting idea initially came from my younger brother, Jack, who is the only person I know who rivals me for love of a caper. But our plan to go with two cousins fell apart before it ever really got going. Still, I couldn't let the idea slide. The more I thought about it, the more boxes it seemed to check.

At this particular time in my journey, I was in the middle of a long period of getting lost in reading and research, and had cleared my wall of the 150 Post-it notes with people's names and replaced them with Post-it notes of recurring themes that appeared over and over again. And every time I'd scan my eyes across them, this insane treasure hunt seemed to be the string that connected them all.

On the base level, it involved a physical activity. Step one for men. But contained in that activity were so many other themes, such as hunting. Yes, males have bonded over hunting animals for millennia, and no, we were not going to kill anything other than possibly ourselves. But still, we were hunting. We were also, in my definition, establishing a tradition, if only because I had already declared that this would be an annual trip in the strange event that we did not find the treasure.

Here's another recurring theme in male friendship: the quest for wealth. The phrase "it could make us rich" triggers in men a reaction similar to that of a golden retriever when they hear the sound of their leash being pulled from the wall hook. Men will practically slobber over themselves to shout "Count me in!" if there's even a whiff of a cash reward with minimal effort. (Women are no stranger to this desire for wealth but possess the intelligence to know this shit never works.)

Toss in a whiff of danger, with the real need to watch one another's backs in the mountains, sprinkle in the outlandish stupidity of grown men dressed as the Goonies, and consider the fact that it would involve a mini road trip in a rental car, and all of a sudden I was sitting on metaphorical gold that I was certain would translate to actual gold as soon as we figured out that damn poem.

I will hear no arguments that this was a bad idea. Let's not divide things into good and bad. Instead, it's better to separate them into "good and boring." And this was not boring.

As a young child watched suspiciously, Matt pulled his Brand costume out of his luggage next to the baggage carousel at the Salt Lake airport. He ducked into a bathroom to change while I used subliminal communication to tell the child not to pull the fire alarm, and when Matt emerged from the bathroom the child was further confused by my excitement. Matt had nailed it—gray sweatshirt cut off at the arms, gray sweat pants with blue shorts over them, a red bandana on his forehead, and the pièce de résistance: one of those coiled chest expander thingies that seemed to exist for about a five-year stretch in fitness culture until people realized they looked dumb using them. I have no idea how he found one, or why anyone would still make them, but I gave Matt an A for effort as we set off through the concourse looking for the Danimal.

He was easy to locate because of course he was wearing his Chunk costume. The Danimal is always game, especially when it involves silly attire, and you don't have to tell him twice to find a red Hawaiian shirt. Dan has a whole array of silly T-shirts that say things like "I'm Dantastic," and he refers to his home in Phoenix as the Dandalay Bay.

Dan was my randomly assigned roommate my freshman year of college, and as he well knows I was initially disappointed to receive a letter informing me that, after I made the somewhat bold decision to leave an Irish neighborhood in Boston and head off for college in the world-away culture of New Orleans, my roommate was a kid from Connecticut named McCollum. I was hoping for someone named Boudreaux or Guillaume; instead, I got an Irish kid from an hour and a half down the road.

But I thank the universe for this accident, for the Danimal is one of the most lovable human beings on planet Earth, and almost immediately rose to legendary status on campus (and I, by nature of being his roommate, caught a ride with him) when he achieved what must be the single greatest feat ever accomplished with a football: He nearly destroyed a 12-story dormitory. He was playing catch in the hallway in front of our room on the tenth floor when he hit a sprinkler head. Somehow, this broke the entire water main, which led to a biblical flood pouring out of the ceiling right in front of our room. Thanks to the laws of gravity, that water did a commendable job of ruining pretty much everything on the floors below and forced the entire dorm to be evacuated for days. I told this story when I was the best man at his wedding.

So now we had Mikey, Brand, and Chunk roaming an airport in search of Mouth. But we did not find Mouth; instead, we found Rob, who greeted us with, "I didn't know you guys were serious about costumes," which is the most Rob move ever. Apparently, the multiple texts about costumes, and the photos of us preparing our costumes, and the text I sent from a store where I stumbled upon a gray Members Only jacket—literally the only thing he needed—had been ineffective in sending the signal that we were indeed serious about the costumes. His lack of costume came as a surprise to no one, for Rob is not a costume guy unless that costume is "Upper East Side preppy." He only veers from this in warmer months, when he switches to "Hamptons preppy." And while he grew up in those worlds, he is both of them and apart from them, "poor" by the standards of someone who could hit a seven iron from his bedroom window to the steps of the Metropolitan Museum of Art. As such, he was a brilliant chronicler of the ridiculous excesses of the rich, my very own F. Scott Fitzgerald. He taught me about Brooks Brothers and the difference between Palm Beach and West Palm Beach, which is apparently very important to know. He also holds the strange distinction of having once looked a lot like Jon Stewart but aging to look a lot like Stephen Colbert. He has been mistaken for both. Among my crew, he's known for another metamorphosis, which is when, as some point during big nights, he transitions from Rob to "Bob," a moment that's easily identifiable by looking at his eyes and realizing that you are no longer dealing with a human but instead a wild animal. I was hoping to see Bob come out on this trip, as it's been a long time since I've run from the police or hidden under a bed in fear. God, I love him. I love them all. It had been too long. Let's go find some treasure!

Our destination was West Yellowstone, Montana, just across the border from Wyoming and the northwest entrance to Yellowstone National Park. It was there, my expert poetry skills had determined, that we would find the treasure near a dry riverbed named Brown's Creek.

To get to West Yellowstone from Salt Lake City meant a solid six-hour ride, most of it through Idaho. This was my first-ever visit to Idaho, and it did not disappoint, because if you asked me to close my eyes and picture Idaho and then say the first thing that popped into my head, it would be potatoes. There are, of course, many majestic mountains and rivers and other strong natural features in Idaho, but none are as strong as the Idaho Potato Lobby, which has made damn sure you think a potato from Idaho is the most gourmet piece of starchy brown dirt you can shovel into your mouth. Which is why the highlight of our journey north was the moment we passed a highway sign informing us that the Idaho Potato Museum was coming up in the town of Blackfoot.

The Idaho Potato Museum was located inside a squat brick structure that could be mistaken for a highway rest stop, and it was perfectly kitschy, with a giant potato statue out front. Inside, there was a lot of very important potato history, as well as a frightening animatronic potato family. Whoever designed the museum was in on the joke that we're talking about potatoes here, and so the museum also contained the World's Largest Potato Crisp, which measured 25 by 14 inches and had managed to survive in its glass case since 1991, when it was made by the people who make Pringles. The crisp did have two small cracks in it, though I suppose that's just part of what makes it great, like a Liberty Bell made from processed dehydrated potatoes.

The mini road trip more than fulfilled its role as one of the icons of male bonding, for there's nothing like getting in a car with the boys when no one knows where the hell you are. There was catching up to do: Rob had just had his first child, a baby girl, and was adorably smitten; Dan was about to start marriage counseling, and we advised him not to lead with "she needs to get her shit together," as he did with us; and Matt was now working for Apple, which is like working at Willy Wonka's Digital Chocolate Factory, so there was much interrogation of what that was like. But it wasn't until we got out of the car and went into that potato museum that it felt like old times, because the only thing to do in a silly museum is to get a little silly, and pretty soon the years melted away and we were the same crew we'd been in our college years, with roughly the same level of maturity. This maturity hit its peak in the gift shop, as we were leaving, when the nice gentleman behind the desk asked where we were from and then informed us they had "free taters for out-of-staters" and presented us each with a carton of Hungry Jack Original Hashbrown Potatoes, a dry potato concoction made, as the label proudly proclaimed, with "100% REAL POTATOES" from Idaho. When life presents you with an innocent group laugh, life has hooked you up, and we were giddy with our free taters for out-of-staters. As we made our way out of Blackfoot, we were in the sort of mood where we immediately stopped for a group photo when we passed a car wash marquee that read: "I call my horse Mayo, and sometimes Mayo neighs." You do you, Idaho.

It was dusk when we finally made it to West Yellowstone, and the imposing Rocky Mountains were barely visible in silhouette as we went looking for our rented house on the outskirts of town. The following morning, after we ate a breakfast cooked by the Danimal that included our "free taters for out-of-staters," we drove just across the Wyoming border to the entrance to Yellowstone National Park. The cobwebs of the previous night's beers were just clearing, and we all shared that moment when you awake in a new place, and that new place is one of the most incredible natural spots on earth, and you share that silent group hug of "How the fuck did we pull this one off?"

We spent the first morning driving around the northeast corner of the park checking out the sites, which meant visiting many things that are trying to boil you to death. Yellowstone sits inside the crater of an active volcano, which I probably knew, or at least once did, but it felt strange to learn it again as we drove around looking at steam blasting from the ground everywhere, reminding you, if you didn't know or had forgotten, that you are indeed inside an active volcano. The Yellowstone Caldera will destroy us all if it goes off again, so if you're reading this, it has yet to happen. In the time we were there, I checked the morning papers each day, which reaffirmed the fact that the place is trying to kill you.

There were stories about two separate hunters being attacked by bears. And there was an awful tale of a dog that went into one of the thermal pools, then an owner who went after the dog, then a friend who went after the owner. The friend lost his legs. The others lost their lives.

As we drove through the park, the boys in the car shared some facts we knew about Yellowstone, which mostly included the fact that we seemed to know very little about Yellowstone. It seemed we had each devoted our pre-planning to doing exactly no pre-planning. I had spent all my preparation trying to decipher a poem with Google Maps.

After our morning sightseeing, we crossed back out of Wyoming to Montana to target a spot named Brown's Creek, because after a lifetime of writing in AP Style I was intrigued by the fact that the word "Brown" was the only word in the poem capitalized as if it were a proper name.

We arrived at a trailhead just across the road from the Yellowstone River, and as we pulled into the parking lot, Rob looked at the mostly bald terrain we were aiming toward, some low hills covered in scrub brush without many trees, and declared authoritatively, "This is not bear country." He had argued against the need for the $50 bear spray Dan and I had each purchased at an outfitter the evening before.

We walked to the kiosk at the entrance to the trail, the thingy that displays maps and recent notices informing you of whichever murderous creature is currently in season, and I will point out that there was no "This is bear country" flyer. Instead, they had engraved that exact phrase into the wood itself, painted in yellow letters at the top of the kiosk, lest a flyer blow away and some asshole from the Upper East Side think "this is not bear country." We had a good laugh about this at Rob's expense, then set out on the trail toward Brown's Creek, climbing on steep switchbacks for quite a ways until we encountered something we wished we had not. It was a deer carcass, though referring to it that way probably causes you to picture a deer. No, this was like if you took a deer made of Lego bricks and then dropped it from a great height. There were hooves in various trees, bones scattered about over a great swath, spelling out in Yellowstone hieroglyphs that this is indeed bear country, motherfucker.

Rob quickly went into defense mode, ordering me to the front with one can of bear spray and the Danimal in the back with the other, because that would clearly solve everything if we came across a pissed-off grizzly. We crept along the trail like the Scooby gang tiptoeing in a dark room, each of us now certain death was about to pop out. Even worse was that our destination, Brown's Creek, was quite a distance off the trail, through some scrabbly terrain we would have to bushwhack. (Forrest Fenn had dropped a hint that the treasure was not near a trail, which made the selection of Brown's Creek feel rather genius when sitting at my computer at home, and rather suicidal now.)

We crept through the brush, shouting, "Hey, bear!" on the regular, as everyone knows that bears do not attack those who refer to them by name. Dan scrunched a plastic water bottle in the back in an attempt not to startle the dreaded mother and cubs. And I became further convinced that Forrest Fenn was a creation of Banksy.

It was unseasonably warm for October, T-shirt weather in the Rockies, and we were sweating and gasping a bit as we acclimated to the dry altitude, but we eventually found Brown's Creek, or at least something that looked like a dry creek bed, and began our search up and down and around, all in that strange task of looking for something, anything, that did not look like it was supposed to be there.

We fixated on the section of the poem that read "If you've been wise and found the blaze, look quickly down, your quest to cease," though we had no idea if that meant, like, a trail marker, or the sun, or whatever. Damn you, Banksy.

After a few hours of going up and down the creek bed we were gassed and ready to exit the food chain, so we went back to the cabin and fell asleep in front of a movie like the old men we happily were.

The following morning, our last full day, we decided to be tourists and go see Old Faithful. As we waited for the eruption on the boardwalk that circles the geyser basin, a bison came uncomfortably close, and we rooted for it to attack the morons who went even closer to take selfies. As for Old Faithful, I won't give you my impressions of this American icon, though I will say the tourist infrastructure around it made it feel a tad manufactured, as if there were Disney engineers behind the curtain.

Instead, I shall give you the Danimal's review.

"D-minus," he declared as we drove away. "Fucking letdown. All it is is steam. Don't fall for the bullshit. There's no huge spooge."

"There was a huge spooge!" I retorted.

"That shit wouldn't have gone over the Green Monster. I don't know what else I can tell you. The Yelp review is a one."

With that out of the way, we steered toward a dam outside the park, playing off Fenn's clue "where warm waters halt." We found nothing, but you already guessed that.

But that night, back at the cabin, knowing we would have to leave at the crack of dawn, the magic happened.

I was searching for a good-bye, and this night took on that special feeling you get at the end of something momentous, an anticipatory nostalgia for this ridiculous idea. Because you know what? It had worked. In every way. The years melted away. We were back to being just as stupid as when we were in college. And, fittingly, we went full stupid the final night. The beer flowed, and I made far too many trips to the garage to pick choice selections from the largest pile of dry, high-quality firewood I have ever had access to. The people we had rented the cabin from had told us to help ourselves to as much as we wanted, so naturally I engaged in a reverse game of Jenga in the outdoor fire pit, attempting to figure out just how high you could stack wood before Smokey Bear showed up and wagged a finger at you.

There were hardly any cabins anywhere near us, and there wasn't a light on in any of them, so we got a tad rowdy and went through the usual routine of drunk-calling our other college buddies and slurring "I love you guys" round the fire. And then, when no one was looking and in fear of our early-morning drive, I pulled an Irish good-bye and snuck off to my bunk bed.

This did not last long, for they found me, turned the lights on in the room, yanked my blanket away, called me a pussy, et cetera. I fought them off once, but a short time later they returned. And you're not going to believe this shit . . . they had girls with them. Twentysomething schoolteachers. I was convinced I was having an alcohol-induced dream, but no, they were real, and had come wandering over from who knows where after seeing our signal fire. Rob had long ago transformed into Bob, and I knew I would have to fistfight him to return to bed, so I pulled my clothes off the floor and returned to fire making and troublemaking, and I'm so glad I did. For those young ladies, who were down from Bozeman for the weekend, told so many off-color jokes that it was immediately apparent that the P.C. Police had yet to arrive in Bozeman. Whatever vision of "Montana schoolteacher" I had in my head—I believe it involved a one-room schoolhouse on a prairie, with a long flowing skirt—was thoroughly turned inside out and upside down by these women who drank and swore like the Southie broads of my youth.

It was the perfect end to the weekend, as was the "can someone drive, I'm hungover" trip down through the majestic Grand Tetons and into the Mormon plains the following day. Dan snored the whole way. The car stank like fast food and farts. It was all so stupid. Perfectly stupid. It was just like being back in our old fraternity house, and if you find yourself saying "fraternities are stupid" right about now, I would say "precisely." Adulthood is too serious. I miss stupid. I need stupid. Being stupid with your friends is guaranteed happiness.

We never did find Forrest Fenn's treasure. I'm highly dubious that it ever existed.

But I have to give Fenn credit. He had lured us into an adventure. And in the process we found our own treasure.

Yeah, I said it. Sue me.

Nine

When my plane landed back in Boston, fall was at its peak: a glorious moment when the leaves turn vibrant hues and the weather is perfect. This spectacle lasts exactly 47 minutes before everything turns the color of death and you must quickly try to remember where you put the rake and your winter coat and why you chose to live in this climate.

To make matters worse, I had taken a leave from my job at the newspaper to work on this book, which meant I spent my days locked in a spare bedroom in my house, reading about loneliness and thinking about loneliness while engaged in the loneliest activity I know of: writing.

After escaping to the Rockies, to my friends, to that great big wide-open land outside my brain, I was now condemned to live inside it, staring at a blinking cursor and a wall full of Post-it notes that I had convinced myself contained some sort of path to an answer. Outside my small window, the world was freezing and dying by the second.

I read a lot of research. I put off reading a lot more. I made grand plans that I failed to execute, and grocery lists that I did, because leaving the house for the supermarket was my rare out-of-the-house-and-away-from-the-damn-computer activity. I also went to the gym quite a bit, which meant I walked in the door a blabbering Muppet of a man, one who had been reading dire news about our broken social connections and clearly needing someone to talk to.

My lonely brain had become consumed with the thought that loneliness was solvable if approached systematically and enthusiastically, but the Post-it notes on my wall clearly told the story of a man grasping for answers. Let's take a quick stroll through them, shall we?

Start a choir—Somewhere in the pile of research was a quote from Oliver Sacks arguing that "we humans are a musical species no less than a linguistic one." This was somewhere in the whole section of research I'd been skimming about humans and music, all of which made total sense and was totally frightening to a guy who was actually kicked out of the fourth-grade chorus for offenses to the aural arts. Just before the Christmas recital, I was politely informed that I would be spending the performance sitting in the balcony, far away from any microphones.

Yet the research on humans and music as a bonding tool was inarguable. It might be the single strongest connector we have, a mechanism in our toolbox that is distinct from those of every other species on the planet. Lots of animals could be said to sing. But humans are the only ones who sing together.

I watched a video of a choir performing Toto's "Africa," which is a hall-of-fame song, but I've never seen it done so joyously. They made the sound of raindrops with carefully arranged snapping of fingers, moved on to a downpour by rubbing their hands together, then jumped and slammed on the risers to mimic thunder. And they looked like they were having the best fucking time doing it, as you could see the group work that had created this beauty.

I went so far as to float the idea of starting a choir to some buddies. Each time the idea was immediately dismissed with "I'm a terrible singer." I would always assure them that it was simply not possible to be worse than me, while pointing out that the beauty of a choir is that the individual is bolstered by the whole. I'd insist that if we hid our bad voices together, we might actually have something approaching mediocre. But my imploring did little to move the needle. Singing was gaaay. Der.

Book Fight Club—Women are great at book clubs. I've never been to a women's book club, but my understanding is this: It's not really about the book. The book is the excuse. But a book club for guys? Repeat after me: gaaay.

So I threw the word "fight" in there—get it?—and floated the idea to a couple of guys. Surprisingly, it didn't get a terrible reception. But it started to feel terribly cliché to buy into the idea that guys can only get together if it involves some sort of aggression. Plus, my gut told me this was not the thing to anchor on, even if I can fight over books with the best of them. Have I mentioned that I was an English major?

Join a men's sports league—Check! For exactly two games, until I had to put "Hockey Billy" back into the closet where he has been safely stored since the mid-nineties.

Mark and I had joined a hockey team Rory had been playing on for a couple of years, and immediately everything felt off. The league played on a rink that was, like, two-thirds the size of a normal rink, and it was four-on-four instead of five-on-five, and there were weird rules about the blue line, and Mark and I were like two old confused guys because this was not the hockey we knew how to play. Plus, we were not nearly as good as our brains remembered us being, and our team was full of much younger kids we didn't quite connect with on account of the 20-year age difference. We got blown out in our second game, and when I called Mark on the ride home, going through all the ridiculous emotions that course through the body after losing a competition—that primordial soup of being mad at myself, my teammates, the referees, the other team, the goalie, and my knees—I told him I was done. I can't overstate how relieved he sounded. He was feeling the same things, and he wanted out, too. It felt like going backward, not forward.

Which was too bad, because I'm envious of the guys who've maintained team sports as part of their life. There's incredible, proven value there. Competition, especially the kind that's a little rough, satisfies some warrior need that's baked into our DNA. Mark and I had high hopes that hockey would satisfy this craving, but the situation was a bad fit, so we choppered out before it got worse. Plus, I'd been reading a little bit of the work by the shame researcher Brené Brown, and she stresses that middle-aged people must take off the armor that they needed to survive youth and adolescence. And something about putting on shoulder pads again wasn't fitting the picture.

Ghana—For pure research purposes, there were three trips I was planning to take, and each failed for a good reason. The first plan was to go to Ghana, inspired by a guy I work with who had told me he'd visited Ghana and was blown away at how intimate the relationships were between men. And the reason for it, he had inferred in his one week as an American tourist, was that the culture did not believe in gay. Like, it was illegal. Like, it was not considered a real thing you could or should be. This is categorically insane, but as a result, he argued, there was no fear of coming across as gay, so a barrier was removed.

I was hell-bent on seeing what life might be like without having to be good and drunk before you tell a buddy you love them. Then I actually spoke to someone from Ghana—he was one of George's friends at Yale—and he told me that my colleague and I had it completely fucking backward. Because it's illegal to be gay in Ghana, men live in fear of coming across as gay, he said. It's not simply a barrier to male friendship; it's a barbed-wire fence. You could get seriously hurt if you dared go near it.

I poked around a little, and read a couple of stories of people being murdered, and realized this was a deadly serious, complex issue, and I didn't want to be just another American tourist who spends a week in Africa and thinks they had some sort of epiphany. So I did not go to Ghana.

Scandinavia—I've never been to Scandinavia. But I like to think I'm someone who pays attention to things that seem to be working in other countries but not in my own, and the Scandinavian countries seem to get so much stuff right that it's almost obnoxious. Add to that the fact that they usually sweep the podium on the list of the happiest countries, despite the fact that their weather is even shittier than the winter I was currently experiencing.

For seemingly every social issue, from health care and paternity leave, to energy and transportation, to care for the aging and care for bicycles, the Scandinavians stare at us from across the North Sea and shake their heads like we're total fucking amateurs. They're also painfully good-looking and stylish. I kinda hate them.

When I learned there was a Happiness Research Institute in Copenhagen, run by a painfully good-looking and stylish man named Meik Wiking who was responsible for the global spread of *hygge*, I decided I'd better hop on a plane and see what this guy was selling. *Hygge*, pronounced "hooga," is a word that doesn't have a direct English translation, but it kinda blends the concepts of coziness and togetherness and contentment and wellness, all of that chewy goodness wrapped into a single word. Think friends sitting around a roaring fire wrapped in soft blankets.

I fired off an email to the institute, with a big ask: I was wondering if I could head to Copenhagen and have Meik Wiking show me *hygge*, help me experience it rather than just having him tell me about it. What struck me most about *hygge* was not that it was a nice concept but that the people actively pursue it. It's an intentional part of their culture. There's a regional obsession with soft lighting and candles and gathering together to be soft as a group. Can you imagine?

Meik was very busy, his assistant informed me, and would be unavailable for an interview but offered me the chance to come join some group that was coming to learn about their work at the institute, which wasn't what I was after. So I did not go to Copenhagen.

Seek Yoda—Here's the thing about a quest. At some point, you start feeling like there's one person, an elder, who holds the key to your journey, who is the person that will point you toward the finish line, to the elixir, the potion, the magic sword that will save you and the people around you. This is not the person who has the answers; it's the person who asks the best questions.

One day, when I was in the shower having warm shower thoughts, I kept picturing the scene in *The Empire Strikes Back* in which Luke Skywalker is dying in a blizzard on the ice planet Hoth and the ghost of Obi-Wan Kenobi appears and tells him he must go to the Dagobah system and learn from Yoda.

And what made that shower thought into something actionable was that in this field of social connections there is most definitely a Yoda. His name is Robin Dunbar. I've mentioned him before. He's the guy behind Dunbar's number, that idea that the human brain can handle only about 150 social connections at a time. He's also the guy who published the study I'd cited way back about how women can maintain friendships over the phone while men need an activity. And there's a million others. Every time I came across some study that had me nodding my head in agreement, it seemed that Dunbar's name was on it in some way. Plus, he was old and cute and a professor at Oxford, and if I had to make a children's book character who was the world's leading expert on friendship, it would be a cute old man who was a professor at Oxford.

So I sent Dunbar a rather gushing email, explaining this quest I was on and asking if I might hop on a plane and come to Oxford to see if he could help me unravel this whole friendship riddle. I mentioned that I was planning to make a few reporting stops in Europe, so as not to seem as weirdly fixated on him as I was. And this was technically true, for at that time I was still planning to go to Scandinavia, and I was thinking of hitting a few places in England, which leads the world in being proactive on this loneliness issue, particularly for their elders. I was most interested in the Silver Line, a 24-hour call center in the northwest of England for seniors who need someone to talk to. I'd read that they get ten thousand calls a day, and what's fascinating is that the people who call rarely ever admit that's why they're calling. Most ask for advice, like on how to roast a turkey. One woman calls every hour asking for the time. Few speak frankly about loneliness. And very few of the callers are men, which is sadly unsurprising.

But my main target was Dunbar, because in my winter writing loneliness I was becoming less and less interested in the Band-Aids for the cancer. I wanted to address the fundamentals. And I had some core questions that remained largely unanswered.

Where did we go wrong?

Are women really better at friendship than men?

Is it possible to reverse-engineer your way to an elixir?

Does psychology really have the answers?

And on a basic level, I craved the advice of a wise elder, so I might ask one of the most timeless and useful questions we have: If you could go back to my age and take some steps, what would they be?

I spent too much time writing and rewriting my email to Dunbar before finally hitting "send" and crossing my fingers.

He did not reply.

I sent him another email, the ol' "Hey, sorry to bother you again, just wondering if you got my last email," which is, of course, the most annoying email to receive.

More crickets.

I naïvely wondered if he was perhaps not getting my emails. He was now listed as an emeritus professor, which is that polite way universities have of saying "retired but kinda still around," so I guessed/hoped he was no longer checking his Oxford email.

So being the hopeless romantic that I am, I decided I was just going to hop on a plane to England and see if I could find this guy, convincing myself that this was how it was supposed to happen, that I had to work for this friendship. Thankfully, when I informed my friend Andrew of this plan, he—being a better journalist and saner human—informed me that I was absolutely nuts. Then he asked me a sensible question that an editor might ask, which was: "Did you try contacting the university's media relations department?"

This is why editors make the big bucks, so I fired off an email to their PR people, got a swift reply, and then, a few days later, a short, polite email from Dunbar saying he was rarely in Oxford anymore, to let him know when I was in Europe, but that it probably wasn't going to work.

The world's leading friendship expert did not want to be my friend. I was back to being a loser, so in desperation I took one last swing, and asked if there was a day I could just come directly to him, wherever he may be, whenever it was convenient.

He did not reply.

So I did not go to the Dagobah system to learn from Yoda.

• • •

Winter had arrived. I'll milk that statement for all its metaphorical worth, for it was so very true. I spent my days writing about everything I'd learned, and my nights wondering why that had failed to translate into anything tangible in my daily life. Many of my old friendships were certainly much stronger than they were when I'd begun this quest, but my day-to-day was exactly what it had been when my stupid editor asked me to write about why men suck at friendship. Work–family–grocery store. The only thing that had changed was that I was now painfully aware that friendship should be a daily priority. So what had been a simple void was now a palpable failure. I had no one to play with, and I knew it.

I stared at the outline of my journey thus far and openly wondered whether it was all for naught. Was my story simply the arc of a man living in a society at a time when social norms made him destined to become a loser, sitting alone in the cafeteria? Were my only "friends" supposed to be the ones on my feed? Was conversation simply something that happened on the podcasts playing in my ears, the shows that always seemed to feature a social scientist being interviewed about how we've never had more tools for connection and fewer actual connections?

I'd been trying to science the shit out of my problems, and it hadn't worked. And the reason for that was simple and painfully apparent from staring at all those stupid fucking Post-it notes. Friendship is not a science; it's a magic, and when it works the mechanism of the trick is unseen by the audience. Two humans come together and a special alchemy turns it into something grand.

Never have we lived in a time with more experts telling us how to strengthen our human bonds, yet never have we lived in a time when our bonds have been weaker. Yale's happiness professor had told me that psychology held the answers, but for every peer-reviewed study telling us one thing, there was a peer-reviewed study seemingly telling us the opposite.

I had relied too much on science, and I'd sucked the magic of creation right out of it. I'd tried to find an algorithm rather than trust the tingles of discovery. Two quotes kept running through my head, both from experts who understood all too well that expertise is the devil of delight. Lester Bangs, the music critic, said that writing about music was like dancing about architecture. E. B. White, the masterful writer and grammarian, said that analyzing humor is a bit like dissecting a frog; it's not a lot of fun, and the frog dies because of it.

So fuck the experts. And fuck my own expertise, because what had succeeded thus far was a story of happy accidents, enabled only by a starting point of willing vulnerability.

Looking at what had most definitely worked (the treasure hunt) and what had most definitely failed (Wednesday Night), I saw they were two sides of the same coin, but the winning experiment had one elementary advantage: a place to go. Wednesday Night was happily low-key, but it died because we never came up with anywhere to go on Wednesday night. The treasure hunt, meanwhile, was an over-structured, over-engineered attempt at a friendship magic trick with all the moving parts exposed. But it wasn't the treasure hunt that made it work; what pulled it all together was the afterthought, the house we rented in the woods to serve as the base camp for the Perfect Male Friendship Adventure. That little house supplied the setting for unstructured play, just like the playground and the school bus and the dorm and the locker room and all those other places that were supposed to be just the staging areas for the larger activities they were connected to. Yes, those big activities brought us together, but it was those in-between places that supplied the glue.

Well, no shit, Sherlock. Everyone knows there's nothing better than getting away with friends, renting a house somewhere for the week or the weekend, and having a sleepover where you stay up too late around a fire. And everyone also knows the chief challenges to such getaways, namely time, money, and fucking *scheduling*.

I knew my friendship problems were not going to be solved by sporadically going on trips. I needed to figure out how to make things work at home, on the daily schedule. When I spoke at South by Southwest, my panel was sponsored by a start-up that had created an app to allow adults to schedule playtime with their friends. While I'd like to think this app will make a billion bucks, I suspect it will die a quiet start-up death, because nothing poisons "we need to hang out" mojo faster than the phrase "let's throw out some potential dates."

So I did not invest in the app.

But I did think seriously about going to Australia.

I called instead. I think this was a wise decision, as Australia is far away, and while I have always wanted to visit and was certain that an escape to summer in the Southern Hemisphere could warm my soul, I had resolved that I would no longer seek to solve my domestic problems by flying international. Plus, on a very practical level, a trip to the other side of the world seemed excessive, for I suspected I already knew what I would find at the Men's Sheds—older guys staying busy by staying busy.

The idea was that simple. Hell, the name told you everything you needed to know about the concept: Men's Sheds. What fascinated me was how something so simple had changed thousands of lives, in ways "experts" never could.

There are two origin stories to explain the Men's Shed phenomenon in Australia, and each one is as simple as it is complex. The first is actually the story of a woman named Maxine Kitto. In the early nineties in a port city in South Australia with the wonderful name of Goolwa, Kitto was running programs at a senior center when she noted the obvious—only women were showing up for her classes. Even worse was that many of those women were being dropped off at the center by their husbands. So Kitto created a space for the men that she called The Shed, and then, most important, she didn't do much else. She didn't create a slate of programming for The Shed. Instead, she left the guys alone and told them to sort it out themselves. Whether this was an act of a social genius or simply the act of a wise woman who didn't want to haggle with cranky old men I do not know. Regardless, it was the key to what is now a global sensation. We'll get back to that.

Kitto's shed lasted as long as her employment at the center, and she moved on with her life unaware that she had left behind the embers of an idea that would become the basis for what is essentially the fourth "men's movement" in modern times, and the only one that isn't inherently awful. We'll get back to that as well.

But first we must address the second origin story, the one with the cranky old man. His name was Dick McGowan, and he was a mover and shaker in a little town in Victoria called Tongala. In 1998, McGowan was thrown out of work, and things were not going well across the board. He was depressed. He'd had an undiagnosed heart attack. He'd had a leg amputated as a result of diabetes, and was using a wheelchair. And when he went to the local senior center in search of some decent diversion, he found the services were not so much an insult to his manhood as they were a misunderstanding of what men actually need. He summarized those needs very succinctly with the statement: "Men need somewhere to go, something to do, and someone to talk to."

On account of being a mover and shaker and all, McGowan got some money from the government and, building off Maxine Kitto's original concept, created a place down behind his aged care center that he called a Men's Shed.

But old Dick McGowan didn't stop there, and I gotta say, only knowing a few things about this guy, I kinda feel like I know him. That being said, I feel like this next move is classic Dick. Just before he died, he got in touch with a reporter for the community newsletter of the National Australia Bank, a little publication that sat on the shelves of every branch, where it was read by old people, I assume. Commerce has evolved to the point where we no longer spend much time waiting in banks, but in my youth I don't recall spending much time reading the bank newsletter.

Regardless, McGowan's shed concept worked, and spread.

And most important? "It was not because of the intervention of experts."

That's Dr. Barry Golding. He's an expert, the last one in this book, I swear. And the chief reason I called Golding down in Australia was because I was looking for some justification to be free of experts, to be let loose with my instincts and intuition.

Golding is a psychologist who studies men and learning, and he just so happened to be doing research in rural Australia as the very first Men's Sheds were popping up. At the moment Golding caught wind of them, there were maybe five or six, and he said he could see immediately that there was something magically simple about the idea—it did not patronize the gents.

"The existing models thought of men as customers or clients or patients or students from a deficit model, the idea that there's somehow something wrong with older men and we need to do something for them. In many ways we're still locked into that model. What Men's Sheds did was empower them to do something for themselves. It didn't dictate what happens inside the space. All it said was 'men' and 'shed.'"

Unstructured. Was it that easy? Was what I really craved simply an organized means of unorganized interaction? "The fact that the Men's Sheds are unstructured is critically important," Golding told me. "If the shed had a schedule and a course they enrolled in, or someone who was in charge, it wouldn't work. It works because men are empowered to do what they want, to come if they want, to participate if they want."

Now let's get back to the idea of the Men's Shed as a "men's movement." It is, but in a way that is very different from the rest, because the formal informality meant it lacked any ideology. Its modern predecessors in that cringe-worthy "men's movement" category would be: the "pro-feminists," whose central premise is that there's something inherently wrong with men that needs to be corrected; the "men's rights" douchebags, who have all sorts of clever ways to avoid admitting they're at war with women; and the mythopoetics of the eighties and nineties, who sought a return to a more primitive, tribal world, with wilderness retreats and sweat lodges and rites of passage and all that stuff. I must confess that I think the mythopoetics were on to something; their chief problem was how many of their adherents believed that this "movement" must exclude women.

The Men's Shed "movement," on the other hand, is blissfully free of dogma. Instead, it follows that basic declaration that my pal Dick McGowan uttered: "Men need somewhere to go, something to do, and someone to talk to." Anything controversial about this statement? No. Isn't that amazing?

If anything, this guiding principle is a shockingly simple way to fulfill Freud's theory of self-determination, which argues that human beings need three things in order to be content: They need to feel competent at what they do; they need to feel authentic in their lives; and they need to feel connected to others. He considered these three pillars—autonomy, competence, and community—to be intrinsic to human happiness.

Golding, who ultimately wrote a book called *The Men's Shed Movement*—he also coined their wonderful slogan, "Shoulder to Shoulder"—has continued to study the sheds as they enter their third decade. And while it's impossible to do any sort of ethical double-blind study to prove the health benefits—which would mean depriving a group of older men of this resource just to prove they're sadder and die earlier—Golding said he's convinced that the men in the sheds are healthier than their peers, and their mental well-being seems to stay stronger longer. "I've interviewed men who have said, 'Without the shed, I'd be dead.' If that's not good data, what is?"

Actually, there's another piece of data that's pretty good: There's currently a new Men's Shed opening somewhere in the world at the rate of about one per day.

I simply needed somewhere to go, something to do, and someone to talk to. I didn't lack for friends; I lacked for a way to be friends with my friends on the regular.

So was a Men's Shed the solution I needed?

Much about the concept was inarguable. I remember reading an article years ago about a playground designer who believed that there were two ideal playgrounds. One was a combination of water and sand. The other was a junkyard. Both were laboratories for unstructured, improvised play.

But the Men's Sheds were not entirely unstructured, in the sense that among their basic rules was the fact that they were open to anyone—including women—and they were geared primarily toward retirees.

What I wanted was a place to play with my existing friends. I had learned, from the many lonely emails I continued to receive in response to my article, that I was not the sort of guy who was willing to become friends with someone simply because they didn't have any. This may make me a bad person, but it's the truth. And what I was envisioning did not involve women because another truth about me is that most of my better friends *are* women. At least in the sense that when I see my female friends it's easier to get into a real conversation, without all the weird masculine baggage and emotional walls. We also seem to keep in touch in more of a real way. When I did that weird thing where I wrote down the names of the 150 friends I actually cared about, it was split almost fifty-fifty between men and women. And my relationships with the women whose names were on those Post-it notes felt stronger than those I had with most of the men. My friendships with women were good. It was the guys who were, in this sense, missing.

For a few weeks after I spoke with Golding down in Australia, all these thoughts were simmering in my head, in that vague space where we shelve ideas that need some external spark to ignite them. My inspiration finally hit late one night as I was lying on my couch, engaged in the important work of scrolling through the endless selections on my television, looking for something that was just dumb enough to quiet my brain and maybe put me to sleep. That's when I started watching the movie *Grown Ups*.

Ten

Among all the *Homo sapiens* in history, I may be the only one who can convincingly utter the statement: "The movie *Grown Ups* changed my life." But that is indeed what happened, complete with a very dramatic lightning-bolt moment.

If you're one of those people who have "taste" or "better things to do with your time," then perhaps you haven't seen the film, so allow me to give you the basics. *Grown Ups* stars Adam Sandler, Chris Rock, David Spade, and Kevin James, who have each been making various versions of the same type of movie for so long that bringing them all together under one tent is a guaranteed way to make a movie that is neither good nor bad but certainly profitable. For there is always an audience for harmless, humorous distraction—exactly what I was seeking on the night in question.

I chose to watch *Grown Ups* over its many competitors in the "happily mediocre" genre because I had actually seen the title mentioned somewhere in reference to middle-aged male friendship. Any specifics escape me, as I was reading a lot of scholarship in that category and can't remember most of it, but that little reference had apparently spun a cobweb onto a shelving unit in the basement of my brain, and then reappeared with just enough force to stop my dumb thumb from scrolling on to the next film.

The movie was just what I'd hoped for—a bunch of juvenile humor that made me happy because I'm more than okay with being the sort of adult who still finds juvenile humor funny. But the usual hijinks were wrapped around an unexpectedly touching plot about a group of childhood friends who return to their home-town for the funeral of a beloved basketball coach. They rent a lovely cabin on a lake where they all reconnect, realize how much they miss one another, and wish they could just live happily ever after in that lovely cabin on the lake.

As soon as I started the movie, I remembered that it had actu-ally been filmed around where I lived. And seeing places you know on-screen is always a strange thrill. In one scene, the friends went to eat at Woodman's, an iconic seafood restaurant—strangely changed to a burger joint in the movie—which was just a few blocks from the location of my derriere at that moment.

As I was watching the scene in Woodman's, the basement lights turned on in my brain again and another tiny cobweb re-vealed itself, and I suddenly remembered something else about the movie, something so incredible that in that moment I could not believe it was real.

I shot up from the couch, put on my shoes and coat, and dashed out the door into the January cold. It was nearly midnight as I pulled out of my driveway with my heart racing, and five minutes later, I parked in a grove at the town lake, home to a tiny beach, two baseball fields, a basketball court, and a small pavilion. It's where my children go to summer camp. I'd been there roughly 1 trillion times. But never, until that moment, had I ventured down a small dirt road that ran from off the back corner of the parking lot into a wooded area.

As I opened the car door and got out, I immediately felt sketchy in that way one does when they imagine having to explain to another human being, possibly a police officer, why they are roaming around in the woods at midnight.

I turned on the flashlight on my phone and made my way down the dirt road, nervous, anxious, every night noise feeling like it was about to kill me, the only nonthreatening sound coming from the crunch of my boots on the frozen earth. About a hundred yards down the road, I could make out a structure on the edge of the lake, and as I made my way closer the moonlight confirmed what, in the eight or so minutes since I shot up off the couch, had felt like a dream.

For there it stood, right in front of me. The cabin from *Grown Ups*.

I had completely forgotten that the cabin scenes had been filmed on the lake, but when it dawned on me I also remembered once hearing that the cabin was actually owned by the town and they rented it out to residents.

When I reached the front porch, I climbed up the rickety wooden steps and pointed my flashlight inside the windows of the main room, which was dominated by a huge fireplace. I don't quite remember my specific reaction in that moment, but it probably involved a fist pump, because that's all you can do when the universe lines up so perfectly.

This felt beyond perfect, a laughably apt answer to this issue that had been taunting me since my flight home from the treasure hunt, this whole simple business of "somewhere to go."

The following day I dashed off a rambling email—I apparently know no other kind—to the town's Board of Selectmen, explaining that I sought to rent the cabin for a "men's group that meets on Wednesday nights." I went on to over-explain such things as how I was inspired by an older crew in town, and how my crew would be men in their forties, "dads who need to get up in the morning"—all of it a not-so-subtle attempt to make clear that we were, on paper at least, responsible adults who would not trash the joint.

Forty-five minutes later, I received a prompt reply informing me that the cottage was closed up for the winter. "Contact us again in the spring and the Board will review your request." This temporary setback was actually a good thing, as it forced me to cool my jets. As the adrenaline cleared from my system, I was pleased to discover that I had already made an important decision. Rereading my email in a calmer state, I realized I was apparently going to combine a Men's Shed with Wednesday Night.

On the last Monday in March, I was given a 7:00 p.m. slot to appear before the Board of Selectmen. The long wait had afforded me the chance to really think about what it was I was hoping to create, and to overthink what I would say to the Board of

Selectmen in an effort to get them to hand over this lovely property for something that sounded an awful lot like a middle-aged
fraternity house.

In the four years I had lived in my small town, I had never actually been to a selectmen's meeting, and was surprised to see just
how small it was, held in a conference room on a middle floor of
Town Hall. I arrived at the appointed time expecting to have to sit
for a bit but instead was called immediately to have a seat at the
end of the long table, with the four selectmen—three men and
one woman, who was the chair—seated at the other end.

And then . . . well, I'm not gonna lie and say I remember exactly what happened next. All I really remember were sensations.
I know words were running out of my mouth very rapidly. I know
my mouth felt dry. I believe I mentioned the original article, and
possibly the New Kids on the Block cruise and Senior Skip Day
and the movie *Grown Ups*. I wanna say they laughed once or twice.
And I remember feeling like the selectman who nodded the most
in agreement as I ran through this long story of the problems with
male friendship was in fact the lone female. She got it. In fact, they
all seemed like they got it. I could feel a tingle inside. It was actually going to work.

Then, in a split second, it all fell apart with a single question,
which I unfortunately answered honestly.

"Do you anticipate anyone will be drinking alcohol on these
Wednesday nights?" one of the men asked me.

I responded that it was not meant to be some drinking event.
The whole point was to find a place to gather that wasn't a bar.
"But yes," I responded. "I imagine some beers will be drunk."

I could hear throats clearing on the other end of the table. I could almost feel the disappointment coming off them, like they were saying, "Dammit, I kinda liked this guy's ridiculous plan. Why didn't he just lie to us?"

Consuming alcohol on town property is not impossible, they explained. It's just really, really expensive. It involves liquor licenses, insurance policies, and the ultimate buzzkill—having a police detail outside. Heck, they told me they liked the idea so much they would probably be willing to waive the $175 fee they charged residents to rent the cottage, but that it would still cost me about a grand per night for all this other stuff.

The energy in the room disappeared. My shoulders fell. It was quiet for a bit. The woman in charge told me she was sorry, and I could tell she meant it. I thanked them for their time, pushed back from the table, and walked out in a daze.

In my gut, I knew it had been too good to be true. Too on the nose. I've been a journalist long enough to know there are no Hollywood endings in real life.

I proceeded to enter a phase that experts describe as "a funk." The movie *Grown Ups* had indeed changed my life; it had derailed it, set it on a stupid path where I'd allowed myself to enter some fantasy land, envisioning this day when I'd invite a bunch of guys to the cottage, push open the doors, and say, "This is all ours, every Wednesday night." Then we would shoot BB guns and sit around campfires and answer important philosophical questions like: "When was the most recent time you pooped your pants?" Then we'd go home to our families and feel better, in ways that would be impossible to explain but easy to identify.

Instead, I was a man without a plan, walking around aimlessly in the early days of April, which is always the most infuriating time of year for me. By this point, I'm beyond ready for winter to be over. It feels like I've earned some sunshine. But winter wouldn't let me go.

I made vague attempts to regroup and rescue the idea for a Wednesday Night shed, but every idea I had seemed like a dead end. Meeting up at a different person's house each week would probably work for about five minutes until it became a giant logistical headache, and it wouldn't feel as free as when you step into an environment that represents neutral ground for everyone. Same would go for renting a room in a bar or something like that; other than the expense, it would never feel like a place of our own, and there would be some buzzkill waiter making sure we didn't light a campfire or shoot BB guns.

I returned to my regular cycle of work–family–grocery store. I didn't know what to do next. I didn't know what I was waiting for. Some magical helper to appear with the answer that would save the day? That's how it works in fairy tales when the would-be hero is cornered and feels like all hope is lost. That shit never happens in real life.

Yet that's exactly what happened to me.

Two weeks after my failure at Town Hall, I arrived in the newsroom one day to find a voice mail waiting on my desk phone. It was from one of the selectmen, a guy named Andy, who had spoken the least during my rambling presentation. His message was brief. He said he'd been thinking about my predicament and that he thought he might have the answer.

A few days later, on a Saturday afternoon, I went to meet Andy at his house, and I spent the short drive with my fingers aggressively crossed, hoping I already knew where this was going.

He lived on a windy road that I had been on many times, and I knew the terrain in that vague way you learn roads you regularly traverse without stopping. I could tell when I was near the beginning, or the middle, or the end, for example. And I really hoped his house was at the end.

As I drove down the road and the numbers ticked by on the mailboxes, I could feel a tingle going up my spine. As my car came over the last rise and his property came into view, I coached myself to calm down, because I was going to need to park and get out and not act like a total flake. But I did allow myself one joyful second to confirm what I had desperately hoped. It *was* that barn.

I parked out front, and Andy came out to greet me. He was about a decade older than me, with a round, friendly face, and after shaking hands and welcoming me he picked up the story he had begun telling me over the phone when I'd returned his message. It basically went like this. He'd grown up down the street, and as a kid he would come to this majestic farm—with its sweeping views of the Essex River snaking through the Great Marsh—and help care for the animals. But mostly, like all the kids in the neighborhood, he would play in the towering barn, which was built in the early 1800s and looks straight out of a New England postcard. When Andy was a kid, the barn functioned as something of an informal community center, and the loft—which ran the entire length of the barn on one side—was like a clubhouse for him and his buddies.

Fast-forward a couple of decades. He had done well in life and was just finishing building his "dream house" in a neighboring town. Then one night he was in a restaurant just up the road eating dinner when he heard that the family who had owned the farm for decades was going to put it up for sale. "I walked straight out the door, drove to the farm, and asked the family what they wanted."

I followed him up the stairs to the loft, as he trailed some half-hearted apologies about how the place was kind of a mess because he pretended not to notice that his teenage daughter and her friends had parties up there. "You have to choose your battles," he said.

When I got to the top of the stairs, the scene in front of me wasn't much. A couple of old couches. Some beat up-chairs. A strand of Christmas lights on the wall. It reminded me of a college apartment, the kind where there's nothing much to break because everything is already broken.

It was perfect.

And the best part was that I didn't really have to say anything. He knew it was perfect. He got it. He'd heard my entire spiel before the selectmen, where I'd gone through great pains to remove any idea that I was looking for a fraternity house.

And then he presented me with a fraternity house.

. . .

Many years earlier, I was in a cafe in Germany, interviewing a famous juggler from Argentina. Long story. Anyway, at one point in our conversation, he told me he had gone for a five-kilometer run that morning, but he had done so while balancing a ball on the top of his head. I asked him why he had done such a thing, and I'll never forget his unapologetic reply: "Because it's nice to think your life is a movie."

This line popped into my head late one Monday night as I drove away from my house with a dozen handmade invitations sitting on the passenger seat next to me. On each of the envelopes I had written "Top Secret" and "For Your Eyes Only." Inside was a hand-drawn map to the barn, along with a date and time. Why did I do such a thing? Because it's nice to think your life is a movie. The fact that it was currently pouring rain outside only made my mission feel more cinematic.

I could have invited the fellas to my new Wednesday Night thingamabob in any number of other ways. But I had chosen this over-the-top route because I needed some comic distance from what I was actually saying, which was "I only kinda know you, but I really like you and want you to join my new club so we can be friends forever." Gaaay.

I pulled up to the first guy's house and opened his mailbox, and as I flipped through my invitations looking for the one addressed to him I stopped for a second and asked myself if I was absolutely sure, because there was no going back after this.

I wasn't questioning whether or not I wanted to commit to

the concept; no, I was questioning the 12 names on the envelopes in my hand. Because from the moment I became convinced the *Grown Ups* cottage would be the answer to all my problems, I had been performing the complicated mental calculus of who I would actually invite to my little experiment.

I had started with the "best friends," guys like Rory and Mark, as well as some other names from my youth—fellas I loved and still felt close to because of our history but never really saw much anymore. I took a step back and stared at the dozen or so names on the wall—yes, I was back with the Post-it notes again—and took a moment to relish just how great it would be to get that crew together in the barn on the regular.

But the more I looked at their names, the more I knew that something was wrong. I loved each and every one of them like a brother. But you can't go home again.

We would be boys forever, but we were not boys anymore. Each of us had gone down a different path, to a different place, and we were no longer a central part of one another's ecosystem. And that was okay. That was life.

I felt no guilt as I removed their names from my wall. They were the definition of friends for life. But I needed friends for my daily life.

So what I felt in that moment was a nervous excitement, a vulnerability, because I wrote down a dozen new names and placed them on my wall, and each of them was a recent friend. I hadn't known any of them for more than seven years, when we moved from the city to Cape Ann. Most I had known for about half that. Some I didn't know well at all. But the one thing they all had in common was that they were part of my new ecosystem and I felt some sort of connection to them, some ineffable spark that signaled that maybe, just maybe, we were meant to be more than simple acquaintances.

Yet as I drove around that night in the rain with their invitations, I was unsettled. I had spent this entire journey trying to get the band back together, but it had done almost nothing to integrate friendship back into my daily life.

Now I was attempting to start a new band, and that's scary as fuck.

Eleven

Wednesday arrived, and I took the day off work so I could pace around my house and cycle through every emotion in my library. Panic, overconfidence, crippling self-doubt, joy, pain, guilt, pride—I did the full workout. Overthinking shit is my favorite recreational drug.

Fortunately, my family was away visiting my in-laws in Virginia, but their absence left the house painfully quiet, and I filled the silence with the sound of a grown man asking himself rhetorical questions aloud: "Why didn't I just tell everyone what I was up to? Why couldn't I just join a bowling league like everyone else? Why does it always have to be so cinematic?"

I felt my stress levels approaching sitting-in-the-chair-before-Senior-Skip-Day levels, for again I was painfully alone and vulnerable, where the only thing that would rescue me was another human being willing to be cinematic, too. But where my previous stunts were just that—gimmicks—this had stakes. This was me declaring I had something to say.

What exactly was I going to say? Good question, and I had begun to address it during my midnight ride to deliver invitations.

That mental draft turned into a full-blown speech that I typed out and printed in the newsroom on Tuesday afternoon. I wrote "Top Secret" on the cover page in black marker, because why stop now.

My Wednesday morning pacing turned into Wednesday afternoon pacing, and at that rate I was still going to be pacing when I delivered my grand speech, which I did not want. So I went to my shed in search of milk crates I could use as a makeshift podium, then drove to a gas station and spent way too much time laboring in front of the beer coolers, for obvious existential reasons. Eventually, the competing factions in my head agreed upon a few choices, and I dumped the beer and some ice into the coolers and dashed to the barn so I could get there 30 minutes early and hurry up and wait.

Andy greeted me when I parked, showed me how to turn off the lights, and wished me luck. He then crossed the street to his house and left me alone with the sounds of the barn swallows and my thumping heart.

You'd think I could remember who was the first person to arrive, but it was all a high-speed blur until I looked around and everyone was there. Within what felt like five minutes, ten guys came up the stairs to the barn, each sporting an expression of bewilderment as he slowly peeked over the railing for his maiden view of the loft frat house. They shook hands and grabbed beers and muttered some version of the theory that I was going to murder them all.

I knew that two of the guys couldn't make it, but other than the obligatory "What the fuck are you up to?" texts, the rest had remained silent and noncommittal. So when my head count landed on ten, I reflexively announced that everyone was here, and something about that statement made all of them go quiet and take a seat as if instructed. Clearly, they were anxious to find out what the fuck I was up to.

"This better be good!" one shouted to a cheer from the rest, and suddenly I was standing in front of a bunch of guys in their freshman and sophomore years of middle age, their faces somewhere between confused and amused. Four were guys I'd met through my kids. Three were guys I'd met through their wives. Three were bros from the gym. And all of them were waiting on me.

I stacked the milk crates onto a card table and made a podium, placed my speech on top, and cleared my throat.

"Allow me to welcome you to the gang bang."

That's probably a joke you're not supposed to make anymore, but it worked. It detonated the awkwardness, and when I began again the group was more relaxed and settled in, which was good, because I started to tell them the story. The whole story. The one you've read here. The one I'd been living. From the stupid assignment, through the messy second act, to the present shift in thinking that had led them to receive a ridiculous "top secret" invitation from a guy many of them knew only in passing.

It's a long story, as you know. It took a while to deliver even the CliffsNotes version, but the guys didn't rush me, and if anything they slowed me down with long digressions, such as when they insisted I stop and go back after I quickly dropped my theory that this all starts with women's hips. There were also many, many breaks for them to take turns busting my balls.

But I could see my confessions finding recognition, and there was an unmistakable feeling that something was happening. That spark. That feeling that this was one of those moments in life that are indistinguishable from magic. These ten dudes seemed to understand me. Now they wanted to understand how this involved them.

I spoke for a moment of the women at my gym, who have a "ladies' night" every single Monday. They would do a workout together, then go to a Mexican restaurant and drink margaritas and solve the world's problems. Enviously, I pointed out how they guarded that night with their lives. They never missed it. Life was scheduled around it. It was their mental health club.

Then I told them about Wednesday Night, and the Men's Sheds, and the *Grown Ups* cabin, as well as the serendipity that had led us to the barn we were in.

"So what am I trying to do here? Why did I invite you guys? Am I starting a fraternity for middle-aged guys? Not really. Maybe. Kinda."

I explained that the owner of the barn had agreed to give it to us on the odd-numbered Wednesdays so that we could come here and . . .

I didn't really have an end to that sentence. What I said in that moment was "hang out," but I had intentionally committed to not being too committed to anything. The goal was to be unstructured. What we would do, what we would become, was up to all who were up for it.

I had, however, committed us to regularity. It was the first thing I'd learned about making adult friendship work, way back in my first phone call with the shrink, and so I'd arranged for us to have the barn on odd Wednesdays. That seemed like just enough to start with, not asking too much of the family calendars, and even a guy could figure out which Wednesdays were the odd ones.

At this point, I was perhaps guilty of putting the cart ahead of the horse. I had been speaking as if they were all interested in the concept. But their faces told me that they really were, so I went ahead and floated an idea I hadn't been sure I was going to mention. It was for down the line, when "Odd Wednesdays" had already become, like, the awesomest thing ever. And that idea was for each of them to bring in a friend of his own, a "pledge class" if you will.

While treating middle-aged dads like fraternity pledges would be spectacularly hilarious, the reason I suggested it was because I wanted to decentralize the group. I wanted, as quickly as possible, for it to stop feeling like "Billy's thing."

But at that moment, it was still very much my thing, and so I finished my time at the lectern with a topic I knew they were all anxious to hear—the question of why I had chosen each of them.

In general, I'm inclusive to a fault. I don't want anyone sitting alone in the cafeteria feeling like a loser. At the same time, my rational brain knew there were limits to that concept. I had become convinced that inviting everyone was what poisoned the Night before Thanksgiving. If I had instead done a small get-together with the people I had been closest to, the ones I actually got together with on those original nights before Thanksgiving, it might have worked. Instead, I'd tried to please everyone and succeeded in pleasing no one.

For the Odd Wednesdays, I had decided to start with a dozen people, plus myself. A Baker's Dozen. I wouldn't blame you if you were groaning right now, but if your name had a number associated with it I would dare you not to feel some affinity toward it. And a Baker's Dozen seemed to fit what I was after, which was not too big and not too small and hopefully just right.

But what was best about committing to a number was that it was a fucking number. It had confines. It forced choices.

"So who is in this room?" I continued. "Well, I had decided I was going to invite a dozen guys, so I wrote a bunch of names on Post-it notes"—I paused here to acknowledge that this was a psycho move, though they didn't know the half of it—"and I moved them around quite a bit until I had the final list. And I must admit that the final list surprised me. I know some of you well, but some of you I only know a little bit. For a few of you, I know your wives much better than I know you. But the common denominator was that you all seem like good dudes. That was it."

I paused here, not because I wanted to let it soak in, but because I could feel that it already had. Of any moment from this entire night of moments, this was the one that felt the best. I had done something vulnerable. I had told a group of guys I liked them and thought we should be friends. But it didn't feel vulnerable. Instead, it felt empowering.

So who was in the room?

I'll start with Gerry, because he was the first friend I made after moving to the area, and it was a case of friends at first sight. We were at a fundraiser for our kids' preschool, and Gerry was the MC for the event, which immediately felt stuffy the way gatherings do when the primary purpose is the extraction of money. Gerry was trying to politely loosen up the place, but it clearly wasn't working. So at one point he went on a quick rant about how the room was too damn stuffy, and I was barely through my nod when Gerry ripped his shirt off. Tore the dress shirt right from his body. Then he just went on with the live auction with his hairy dad belly bouncing in the wind. There was some uncomfortable laughter, but I think my wife and I were the only ones who found his stunt genuinely funny. It wasn't obnoxious in the "look at me" sense; no, it was more of a playful scold, as if to say, "Look at you. Remember when you weren't so uptight?" When the auction was over I went right up to him and made my first dad friend at the preschool.

I'd actually invited three dads from the preschool, which is funny in retrospect. One of them was Andrew, who I had already become close friends with after convincing him to drink the Kool-Aid and join my gym. The other was a guy named Ryan, who went to art school and made robots for a living and was the first guy I sorta hung out with after moving to Cape Ann. Naturally, I'd met him through his wife. Ryan and Andrew had independently become kayaking buddies, so the three of us were kind of a unit, but the sort of unit that rarely got together. This would hopefully change that.

Next, the three gym bros. There was Brian, who was the strong,

silent type who didn't say much of anything to anyone, but we connected somehow, largely because he was a *Globe* subscriber, which
meant he had regular complaints he wished to lodge. There was
Kevin, who I had liked immediately for those great reasons that
can only be described as indescribable, and we had become practicing friends when he invited me to join a crew that occasionally
played bar trivia on Tuesday nights. And there was Jon, who owned
the gym with his wife. Jon and I shared a ton of interests in common, which is classic friend-making material, but what had actually pushed us past the acquaintance category was an even more
powerful kindling: conspiracy, in the form of the mutual dislike of
a third person. When that person's name had come up randomly
one day and we each reflexively took a look around and dropped
our voices, we were off. As they say, the enemy of my enemy is my
friend.

Through Jon, I had met Rob, who was his best friend growing up, and who had children who went to school with my own.
Our youngest children were in the same class, which was great
because, as any parent will tell you, you tend to make most of
your connections with other parents if their oldest is the same
age as your oldest. Rob was a great dude, and we shared a very
"small world" connection in that he owned a two-man construc-
tion company. When we met, the other man was the husband of
the woman who is perhaps my closest friend at work. That guy
ultimately left to become an art teacher, and in his place Rob had
hired Scott, who was the husband of one of the women in my
wife's crew in town. We had always gotten along well, so I invited
Scott, as well as Tom, another husband from that crew who was

in the same category—good dudes that I had spent enough time with to be slightly more than acquaintances but not enough to be actual friends.

And finally, there was Steve, who I'd been most nervous to invite. I knew his wife from the gym, and had met him only a handful of times. But he seemed like a great guy, and we shared something cute in common: He had grown up in the house I now lived in.

If you can judge a man by the company of the friends he keeps, I would say I'd done all right. And after I finished quickly introducing everyone, I had officially run out of things to say, so I nervously filled the air with the ol', "If there are no further questions, then let's sign our names in blood."

I got a laugh, but then came a silent pause, just long enough for that familiar feeling of panic to start creeping up my spine. I had thrown my personal saga out there, all of it, and in that silence it just sat there, naked for all to see. And I suspected they would now have many questions about this bombshell I had just dropped on their heads on a school night.

But no one asked any questions. No one stepped forth to bust my balls. That would all come later.

No, what they did in that moment is something I will never forget. They gave me a very sincere round of applause.

The following morning, I woke up at 4:30 a.m., something my brain likes to do to punish me on mornings after I've had too much to drink or too much to think. I'd had both.

I had promised Andy that we'd be out of his barn by 9:30, but when I finally thought to check the time it was already 10:30 and we were still going strong. The beer was running low, but conversations were still pouring forth, and no one seemed to be moving toward the door.

Whatever this was . . . it had worked. It had fucking worked.

But would it work again? That's what had my brain twisted into a Möbius strip as I resumed pacing my house the following morning. As you've no doubt gathered, I can go a couple of rounds with doubt and second-guessing, but I wasn't second-guessing the night. My whole quixotic journey had led to this point, and when I finally spilled it all out, the response had exceeded my expectations. There was magic in the room. That's a great feeling. But it's a transient feeling. And what had me pacing again was the question of how to repeat it.

When we finally called it a night and said our good-byes until the next Odd Wednesday, I could already sense a gaping hole in my plan. We had great people. We had a great place. Now we needed a great purpose. Somewhere to go, something to *do*, someone to talk to.

As the universe would have it, my own newspaper had published an article that very morning by a social psychologist with the headline: "Looking for happiness? Try purpose instead." I had already read quite a bit about purpose, for it lives in the same space as friendship and loneliness—it's an area where a mental and emotional state can have startling effects on physical health. As we've seen in the Blue Zones, having a reason to get up in the morning, a belief that your life has meaning, can make you measurably healthier. Purpose is essentially Aristotle's definition of happiness.

But if purpose for the individual can be defined as the reason to bounce out of bed, on a group level it's the reason to show up day after day. I had intentionally left this space blank for Wednesday Night. I knew we needed a purpose, but I was hoping it would come organically, as a group.

Yet as I paced the following morning, I worried that we needed to find a purpose sooner rather than later. Saying good-bye to the fellas, one of them had asked, "So just come back here in two weeks and we'll do this again?" He said it without agenda, just wanted to make sure he understood the plan. But it had me wondering if I understood the plan.

There's a ton of evidence on the benefits of sitting around and talking, and that is basically all we had done. Which was great. But since it was all we had planned to do, it was a problem. Without an activity to put men into that shoulder-to-shoulder position, we were at risk of feeling like the barn loft was for co-rumination, which is a fancy way of saying sitting around and talking about our problems. Men instinctively avoid that shit like the plague, for it is just as infectious. Science has proven that listening to a downer makes you down. No one has space for that sort of emotion except in the case of very close friends, and we weren't there yet.

I was getting ahead of myself—shocker, I know—and the third pot of coffee wasn't helping. Eventually, the rest of the world awoke and my phone started to light up with messages from the fellas. Everyone was stoked. Everyone was in. Everything would work itself out, right? Put down the coffee and take a shower, dude.

Twelve

For the next two weeks, it was all good. When I'd run into one of the fellas, it was hard to keep from giggling. The whole thing felt ridiculous and awesome. And the "secret" was certainly out, for several of their wives, as well as a few of their children, attempted to interrogate me about the thing in the barn. "What happens in the barn stays in the barn" was my reply; not the most original joke, but if it ain't broke, don't fix it.

As our next Odd Wednesday rolled around, I wondered if I needed to send out a reminder. The point was that it was always on the schedule, but maybe a reminder for this first one was in order. Then I heard from one of the guys that he couldn't make it due to a preschool graduation, which was actually good because it meant he knew it was happening and wanted to come, right? Ah shit, I was nervous again.

That Monday had been Memorial Day—you know, the alleged start of summer—but it was so damn cold on Wednesday night that we would have frozen to death in the barn. What was good about that is that the group text got fired up naturally as we looked for an alternative, and Kevin offered to host at his house, which was good because it meant we could also watch the Boston Bruins, who were playing in the Stanley Cup final that night. A few people texted to say they couldn't make it because several end-of-school-year events were going on, and it ended up being just four of us.

But that was perfect for sitting in a living room, because as I've previously mentioned, four is thought to be the perfect number for a conversation. Plus, one of the guys who came was Steve, who I knew the least going into all this. But he had taken the leap and shown up, and the smaller crowd gave us our first real chance to talk about more than the fact that he'd grown up in my house.

Gerry also came, wearing a shirt, unfortunately. And of course there was Kevin, who was already an active friend for me, thanks to the fact that we both loved bar trivia. We had certainly become friends at the gym, but it took that simple extracurricular to put us in that shoulder-to-shoulder position on the regular, the two of us hunched over a piece of paper trying to remember the name of the actor who played the bad guy in *The Karate Kid*.

That's all it took for us; friendship is complicated unless it's painfully simple. And that's what I had to keep reminding myself when I'd feel my brain racing ahead, convincing myself that Wednesday Night would collapse without some grand purpose, something to commit to.

At the moment it was still simple. Just a couple of guys sitting around watching the Bruins. And simple was working.

·   ·   ·

The weather finally warmed, and we moved from the barn to a spot on the edge of the farm, where we set up a fire pit on a spot overlooking the river that runs through the salt marsh. It was a ridiculously scenic spot, far enough from Andy's house to feel completely private. Most everyone made it out for the third Wednesday, and there was a primitive pleasure in sitting around a fire at the end of a day, cold drink in hand. We had some good laughs, but what I remember most about that night was that near the end, when it had finally become pitch-black, there was a good long stretch where we all just stood around the flames, watching them dance and saying nothing.

The good vibes rolled into the summer. We spent more nights in the barn and around the fire, shooting pellet guns at empty cans. Another night we went paddling around the offshore islands, a flotilla of kayaks and paddleboards. Then at the end of July, I took off for two weeks with my wife and kids and the fraternity took a little break. At least that's what I thought.

On the first Odd Wednesday after I returned, I sat in the barn loft for a solid hour before I admitted to myself that no one was coming. Even worse, I was kind of glad, because I hadn't really wanted to go myself. I was tired in general. And I was tired of having to be the cheerleader every other week. It felt like I was forcing it; everyone still referred to it as my thing, rather than our thing. And the one area I had intentionally avoided trying to force—the activity, the thing we were actually going to do, the purpose— had yet to magically appear. We were essentially gathering to sit around and talk, and I knew that was only going to fly for so long.

Two weeks later, an Odd Wednesday came and went. I never

mentioned it. Nor did anyone else. If anyone showed up at the barn that night, I didn't know because I had fallen asleep on my couch alone.

I ran into Andrew at the gym one morning and we had a long talk about the whole situation. Which was good, because he's rational in ways that I will never be—he's the one who had convinced me not to fly to England to ambush an elder professor and beg him to be my friend.

As we stretched after our workout, he gave me a pep talk about how I should be proud of what I'd started, even if this was it, even if the club failed. The relationships that had begun there would not. He's an articulate and convincing son of a bitch, and I spent the next couple of hours doing my best to look on the bright side. There was no doubt that my friendship with each of the guys was stronger because of this initiative. That included the two guys who never returned after the first night. One was Tom, the husband of one of my wife's closest friends in town, who admitted that he was kind of socially awkward in groups and a homebody in general. But he confided this to me as a friend would, and we've hung out a few times since then, round the fire pit in his own backyard while our kids played loudly around us. The other was Brian, the quieter guy from the gym. I didn't think he was a group guy, but I invited him anyway and fully expected he might never come back, which was correct. But when I do see him around, it feels, in the tiniest of ways, like we're closer.

To each of these men, I had announced "I like you," and that's surprisingly daring in male friendship. At the same time, it's scientifically proven that people are more inclined to like you if they know you like them. We kind of understand this intuitively, but we rarely go there, as it comes across as an act reserved for when you *like* someone.

With those dozen guys, I had spilled the secret: I like you and I want to be better friends with you. And guess fucking what? It had worked. I was certain they also liked me, for they each spent a considerable amount of time going out of their way to make fun of me. Not to brag.

The calendar rolled over to September. The kids went back to school, and the nights got shorter and cooler. We had gone the entire month of August without a gathering, or at least one that anyone attended other than me, and as the first Odd Wednesday of the fall arrived, I wasn't sure what to do. Then, just before 2:00 p.m., Kevin texted the group. "Fight Club tonight?" He was great like that. He was the first to say "I'm in," and had been the most active about keeping the group together.

It would ultimately prove to be a night that was bad for everyone's schedule, but we had reawakened, and the texts flew back and forth. I had spent the day working on this book, and when I mentioned this in the group text, along with the quip that it culminated with the Worst Idea I've Ever Had, I was clearly fishing for some guidance. It arrived, as it should have, with the group calling me out for being a drama queen. Yet an important conversation had begun, and I was told that I was being overly critical (Kevin);

that summers were tough (Jon); and that I drank horse semen (Rob). Then the great Gerry dropped in from the clouds with an all-time text.

We hadn't heard from Gerry in quite some time, which surprised me, as he'd clearly had an emotional connection to the gesture from day one. Early on, he'd dropped me a late-night text out of nowhere that read: "Billy, Thanks for giving a fuck. Honestly." He was good like that. No, he was great like that, and on this night he shone.

Hey Odd Wednesday guys and Billy, this is Gerry. Horse semen and Billy's beautiful depression aside, I think this idea was intriguing, if not necessary and worthy. I'm thankful. I'm still on board. Billy, your original Globe article defined the idea that men 1. Bond over a goal, and 2. Take care of their families. Stop acting like this is a failure. I will help any of the men I met in the 'barn' on the initial night move a couch or get to the airport. In the meantime just like the rest of you I'm trying to balance being a dad and husband and dreamer. At the moment I'm at a bar in Haverhill waiting for my daughter's practice to be over. I love you all.

It was exactly what I needed to hear, what we all needed to hear, especially the reminder of step 1: Bond over a goal.

As the texts wrapped up for the night, we resolved that everyone would show up in the barn in two weeks' time to figure out what that goal was.

. . .

In 1941, a Swiss engineer named George de Mestral was walking through the woods when he noticed that both his pants and his dog were covered in burrs. Most people who have experienced this have responded by simply saying "fuuuccck." But de Mestral was the sort of person who filed his first patent at the age of 12 (for a toy airplane), so after he said "fuuuccck" he went home and looked at one of the burrs under a microscope. He wanted to figure out how it could attach itself to fur and fabric with such strength, yet come off with moderate pressure. What he observed were tiny hooks, thousands of them, which triggered an idea. After 14 years of trial and error, he finally succeeded in creating a synthetic version of those tiny hooks, which he called Velcro.

All through my journey, I'd been struggling to come up with a term for what it was that bonded people. It was something easy to define in retrospect; you could look at almost any great friendship and point at that thing that anchored it. But when trying to purposefully engineer that thing—the story of the last several years of my life—I could never give a name to what I was looking for. It remained, for lack of a better term, "that thing."

The word "Velcro" had run through my head a few times, as it was the closest descriptor I could find: Two pieces strongly attached yet easily pulled apart. But the word itself felt too industrial, too scratchy to the ear, and failed to capture the softness of human friendship.

As our barn summit approached and I was back to brooding about what "that thing" might be, I read the story of the inspiration that led de Mistral to create Velcro, looking for some inspiration of my own. When I learned that he had arrived at the name Velcro by combining the French words *velour* and *crochet*, I knew I had found it.

In English, that translates to "velvet hook."

Ruth and Judy. That's the first thing I thought of when I read the words "velvet hook."

I first met them after Ruth wrote me a letter. She was about to turn 70 and said she had been reading my articles for years and sensed that I might be the person to tell the story of her friendship with a woman named Judy.

They had met in the 1970s when Judy placed an ad in the local newspaper, looking for moms to join a playgroup. Ruth showed up, and they immediately hit it off, discovering that they shared a love for old bicycles, which they started sneaking off to ride for an hour here and there. That morphed into daylong trips and then overnights, and soon they were lugging Blukey and Brown Bear—as they nicknamed their bicycles—onto planes and trains and boats to explore Iceland and Ireland and Holland and every square inch of the northeast coast from Rhode Island to the tip of Nova Scotia.

When Ruth wrote to me, it was because something had changed in their story. Age had come with ailments. They'd both survived breast cancer. Blukey and Brown Bear weren't seeing much action, and they could sense that this chapter of their lives was coming to an end. So they started a new beginning—they went electric.

For two days, I chased after them on Martha's Vineyard on their first grand adventure on their new e-bikes. They were chatting and laughing and having the time of their lives while I struggled to keep up. They were like two kids on a caper. Heck, Judy had even booked us rooms at a youth hostel. Their relationship was a joy to watch, and of course it was about a whole lot more than their bikes. But they recognized that bicycling was what connected them. It was their thing. It was their velvet hook.

All of a sudden, I could see velvet hooks everywhere. There was a crew of guys I'd written about who had played street hockey every Sunday morning since 1970 in front of the house where one of the guys grew up, and the pond hockey tournament Rory and his college buddies played in every winter on Lake Winnipesaukee in New Hampshire (I'd been a sub the last two winters). In both instances, the hockey itself was terrible; it's hard to play smooth on a street filled with traffic, or on a frozen lake with huge cracks in it. But it was the velvet hook.

My own life was littered with velvet hooks, those connections that revolved around simple things like playing bar trivia or surfing. Even more so, I could see what happened to friendships when a velvet hook came undone. I had once been rather close to two guys named Will and Scott, who lived right around the corner from me, and the three of us, for reasons that don't add up in retrospect, had created a fantasy league around the reality show *Survivor*. Every week we'd go to Scott's house and watch the show and horse-trade humans in real time. This went on for years; then we all moved to different places and the Velcro came undone.

Then there was the one that was so small but meant so much, with my cousin Michael. He's about 20 years older than me, and I always looked up to him. He lived in the apartment below mine when I was growing up, and when I was eight or nine he told me he was going to run the Boston Marathon. This was an interesting decision, because he was not a runner and the race was, like, a month away. When marathon day rolled around, I went with my family to a spot around mile 16, at the beginning of the notorious Newton Hills, and when Michael finally came by he looked like death. There was no way he was going to survive another ten miles. But that's exactly what he did. Years later, he would tell me the only reason he was able to finish was because he saw me and my younger brother, knew how much we looked up to him, and knew it would break our hearts to see him fail. The moment he told me this was the moment I decided I had to run the Boston Marathon, which was an interesting decision because I was not a runner. But I did it, which in turn inspired Michael, now in his sixties, to run it again. When he did, I waited for him atop Heartbreak Hill, the most infamous spot on the course, with a handmade sign that read: "Heartbreak Is Behind You Now."

The sign now hangs in his office, and we made a pact to watch the race together each year atop Heartbreak and hold the sign together. The only exemption would be if one of us was running. Of course he's run it every year since, so the only time we actually see each other is atop that hill when he stops to hug me. But it's incredible. It's our velvet hook.

. . .

Before the next Odd Wednesday, I did something I should have done a long time ago. I called Ozzie, the guy who had first told me about Wednesday Night, for it occurred to me that I had never actually asked him what the original crew actually did on Wednesday nights.

"We always try to have an activity," was the first thing he said, which I both needed to hear but also didn't need to hear. "In the summertime, if the weather is good, we go sailing. A couple guys have sailboats, so we do that a lot. We used to do some mountain biking. It varies, but we always try to base it around an activity.

"In the wintertime, one of the guys has an amazing barn." (See: needed to hear/didn't need to hear.) "Inside the barn he has a shuffleboard table and a pool table, and there's this badminton-type game we play. People just show up, and there's always something to do. We don't just sit around."

He said it all in that quick way people use when their tone is meant to tell you there isn't much to tell you. Just somewhere to go and something to do.

Ozzie and I made tentative plans for me to come to one of his Wednesday Nights, and I hung up feeling like the answers were incredibly simple but painfully complicated. Or maybe I just couldn't help but make them so, because I had already been toying with an idea for an activity that involved the barn in winter and the ocean in summer. And that was to build a boat.

Essex, the town I live in, was once the "shipbuilding capital of the world." That was back in the era of schooners, but there were still a few boat barns around town, and they were filled with groups of old guys futzing around and occasionally building a boat. So there was something romantically fitting about the concept. But it was deeply complicated, of course, as I had no clue how to build a boat, and it would require big expense and commitment. Not to mention that it would mean approaching Andy and saying, "I know you said we could use the loft in the barn every other Wednesday, but can we take over the whole thing all winter?"

The boat I had in mind was a pilot gig, which is a big rowboat that seats six, plus a coxswain. I knew some women who rowed them, and they would get together a couple of mornings a week and have a grand old time on the ocean. It seemed like something worth copying, but the rowing club they were in had a limited number of boats and heavy demand, which is why I had the idea that we could build one through the winter and then row it in the summer. But when I floated the idea to a couple of the guys, it never got a grand response. And I could guess why, or at least I knew the reason that I was never in love with the grand proposal. It wasn't a velvet hook. No, starting something like that from scratch was a steel handcuff, another task-heavy commitment for adults who were piled high with them.

When Jon first mentioned the idea that we should build a pump track, I certainly didn't think it was the plan that would save the group. Instead, my response was: "What the hell is a pump track?"

Jon was the guy who owned my gym and became my friend

after we discovered we shared a humorous distaste for a mutual acquaintance. Just like that, we were junior-level confidants sharing an honest whisper beneath the pleasantries that live above. Our path to actual friendship accelerated rather quickly from there, because we saw each other a couple of times a week at the gym—checking off both consistency and activity—but also because we seemed to have in common a strange number of very particular interests. One of them was BMX cruisers, which is a rather specific and somewhat obscure type of bicycle, an oversized BMX bike for oversized children. I had purchased one years before as a thirtieth birthday gift to myself, a promise to never really grow up, and every time I so much as look at it I feel the urge to jump a curb.

At some point during that summer, Jon had discovered there was an old BMX track about 30 minutes away, and we'd taken our kids there one Saturday morning to watch the races, which wasn't all that much fun because it's rather difficult to be next to a BMX track and not have a chance to ride it. My boys immediately began planning a return event when they would bring all their friends and actually ride. Such is the pull of dirt jumps on a child's heart. A few weeks later, we returned with their friends, and the verdict was that it was pretty much the best day ever. I think the adults had more fun riding than the kids, especially this adult. I got, like, three feet of air one time.

So when Jon told me that a pump track is "like a BMX track, only it fits in a much smaller area and is like a roller coaster for your bike," I very much liked what I heard.

• • •

It took about 18 seconds to convince the rest of the fellas. Most everyone had shown up at the barn for the what-are-we-gonna-do summit, and I ceded the floor to Jon, who quickly explained the idea, and it was settled without really needing to say so. Sure, let's build a pump track. We moved on to having a few beers and a few laughs after agreeing that I would be stuck with the small task of convincing the town to give us some land and maybe some earth-moving equipment.

Would we ever actually build a pump track? I had no fucking idea. But it was a nice, soft velvet hook, and exactly the level of juvenile we needed. The thought of getting out the shovel and building some sweet jumps hit all the right notes with the inner child, and by saying we were going to do it we felt like we had settled the unsettled feeling and could move on. What I remember most about that night is a moment when I was laughing, and with that laugh came a millisecond when it felt like a huge weight just lifted from my shoulders. It had been two and a half years since I'd walked out of that editor's office, and ever since then I'd been racing to fix something that had broken simply because I wasn't paying attention to it. What calmed me in that moment was the certainty that I would never let it slip from my attention again. I would always keep an eye on it, but it no longer felt like something that commanded my full attention. And as I looked around at the gentlemen in the room, I daresay I had infected them as well. They, too, were keeping an eye on it in a way they had not before. And it's easy to relax if you feel surrounded by people who are looking out for you.

Earlier that afternoon, I had received a surprise phone call from Ozzie. I could tell immediately that he was somewhere super windy; I could also tell that he may have had a few drinks in him.

"We wanted to tell you that we changed Wednesday Night and it's now Wednes*day!*" he yelled, and I could hear laughing around him as he again emphasized Wednes*day*. He was on a sailboat with his crew, and I gathered that they had been discussing my request to attend, for in the background I could hear them shouting things like, "Tell him he needs to bring some good tequila if he wants to come. And I mean *good* tequila!"

There was some chatter about when I might come, but I knew in that moment that I never would, because I didn't need to. Just listening to these grandfathers acting like teenagers, I knew there was nothing I needed to see, for there was nothing *to* see. Wednesday Night was not an event. It was a promise. Their main activity was to show up for one another. To show intent. That was the science of Wednesday Night.

Thirteen

"**Y**ou got a second? I've got a couple questions you would be perfect for."

I was standing in the office doorway of the magazine editor who had gotten me into this mess, and he looked up from his red pen and let out a giant laugh. Francis had left the *Globe* immediately after he had lured me with claims of an assignment I'd be perfect for, moving to a more relaxed gig as the editor of a college alumni magazine. I suspected my assignment and his move were related, but his quick disappearance meant we'd never had a chance to sit down and unpack it.

Then he surprised me by coming back. After being gone for a couple of years, he had returned to the *Globe* as the top editor at the magazine, which is a good gig if you want to do great journalism and surrender all your free time.

"Have a seat," Francis told me, brushing aside the proofs on his desk.

The last time I had accepted an invitation to have a seat in his office, I had no idea that my life was about to change. I was here now to thank him for the fact that it had. But I also wanted to get to the bottom of something I had never bothered to ask when he first started waving all this data in front of me to make the argument that men had no friends and it was a public health crisis. Namely, why was *he* pulling all this evidence together?

He let out another laugh. If I had to describe Francis in a single sentence, I'd say he's an easy laugh. And this laugh said: You caught me.

"You know that saying 'News is what happens to editors'?" he said, then let out his biggest laugh yet. "I just felt myself not making time for friends. Ever. And I thought, 'What will it be like in twenty years?'" We were the same age, he said, with young families, and he made the easy bet that I might sense the same things creeping in. "I wasn't exactly lonely, but I had reached lonely potential," he said. "It was this feeling, and then it was 'Are other people feeling this?' You know how sometimes you notice something in your life and then all this stuff starts resonating and you notice it in a way you maybe wouldn't have before? So I think I felt it, and then I saw the Surgeon General's statements, and I started wondering if there was something here. I was testing my own feelings. 'Is this just me, or are there other people feeling this way?'"

Answering yes to that question had clearly changed the direction of my life. And so I asked if it had done the same for him.

"That's the key question. I've thought a lot about that. And it's complicated. And me coming back here further complicates things. It would be a much easier story line if I were still someplace else." He shrugged. After he left, he said he made big plans, reached out to some old friends about getting together, and generally vowed to have a better work/life balance.

Then he paused for a moment. His face changed. The joy of that decision had run into that thing we call reality. "I wasn't one hundred percent successful," he continued, "and part of what I realized is I'm sort of built this way. I put everything into the job. So it's a harder habit to break than I expected it to be."

There was more than a bit of guilt in his voice. It's the catch of life. Putting time into one thing means taking time from everything else. The ideal goal is to "have your priorities in order," but that concept oversimplifies something that's subjective and fluid. Perhaps a more realistic goal is to identify your priorities and make sure that none are being neglected. For him, leaving the mission of hard journalism for something softer was neglecting something that was important to him. So this second go-round was to prove he could have that without neglecting the rest. And he had a head start because he was simply aware.

"While I was gone I took up golfing," he said. Pause for extended laughter on both sides of the table. "But golfing is just the excuse," he continued. "One of the things you said in your story, which I had never heard before but will remember forever, is about looking at the world shoulder to shoulder. What I looked forward to was having time to bullshit with my friend Kyle, and golf was the thing that kept our hands busy while we were talking about kids and what's going on at home."

His return to the world of deadline journalism had meant less time on the links, but I was glad to see he was clearly hustling to make it work when it could. "Last weekend, on Saturday night, Kyle and I went to the movies. We went to a ten-thirty showing, which is like my bedtime, but we left at nine when the kids were going to bed, went out for a quick drink, shot the shit there, went to the movie until twelve thirty, and then I dropped him off. It was like a date, and it was great. And I feel like I'm doing things like that because so much of what you wrote about has stuck with me ever since. It wasn't like a switch you could flick and it was all fixed. There's still lots of work to do. But just having some language to go with it makes me more aware of it."

That was it, in a nutshell. Good editors are like that. You can pile them high with a tangle of thoughts, and they will help you find the spine of a story.

There would never be a "happily ever after" moment in my quest. No potion to bring back that would save everyone. No switch you could flick and all would be fixed. There would always be work to do. But I had the language, and maybe even some tools, to stay on top of it. And Francis commended me for using the simplest tool of all.

"You're showing up. It's true what they say: Ninety percent of life is just showing up. No one cares if you have something articulate or new to say; just being there for your friends is what matters. That's something I've learned on this journey I kind of started with you. It's just about being there, and saying 'It's nice to have you as a buddy' matters a lot to people."

"Well, I consider you a buddy," I said to him, "and I'm glad you're back here."

I have a start-from-scratch fantasy. Sometimes it comes to me in dreams where I'm offered the opportunity to go back to some point in my past and redo my life, only this time without screwing up so many things. Other times, it manifests in the real world, such as when a former co-worker I barely knew lost all of his possessions in a fire and I nervously asked him—in the office bathroom, of all places—if there wasn't something great about having to buy all new socks and begin again. He confessed that he was finding the entire experience liberating, though his face told me he felt like he wasn't supposed to say it out loud.

Thankfully, life has a cure for such do-over fantasies. It's called raising children.

Now, I have largely resisted, in these pages, the desire to hand out hard advice. The only unsolicited advice I'm comfortable doling out is: Don't give unsolicited advice.

I'm good with questions but shy away from answers, because friendship is a matter of the heart and thus there are no actual "experts." To illustrate this, I'll point out again that we've never had more peer-reviewed "expertise," yet we've never had more people who feel such a disconnect. There is guidance in the studies, for sure, and the dire data about loneliness and its effects should be taken as a call to action no less serious than bad blood work. But there are few clear prescriptions for cures, and knowing is not half the battle. Gaining awareness of the incredible dangers of isolation, and the health miracles of strong connections, is certainly the first step, the call to action. But every other step in achieving friends for life is really the story of intent—having it, showing it, and prioritizing it in your daily life.

Raising children, however, demands the daily dispensation of guidance. Much of it is mundane: "If you just left your shoes near the door, we wouldn't have to spend all morning looking for them." Much of it is in the simple service of keeping them alive: "I wouldn't stick those scissors in that socket if I were you." But there are also many deeper moments when you have the opportunity to advise them on how you would do things differently if you could go back and do it again. It's like delivering a miniature commencement address to an audience strapped in car seats.

"What should young people do with their lives?" That's a good question, and the writer Kurt Vonnegut once came up with a good answer.

"Many things, obviously," he said. "But the most daring is to create stable communities in which the terrible disease of loneliness can be cured."

The world my children will grow up in is much different from the one I was born into, and so my commencement addresses are delivered to them as individuals but also as members of an as-yet-unnamed generation, one that I'm calling—both for encouragement and as something of a dare—the Villagers.

Born after Generation Z, the Villagers took their first breaths in an era that began with the election of Obama and continues through Trump, a world where social possibility and social division seem to go hand in hand.

Thankfully, it's a world where old wrongs are being righted. But it's also one where old lessons are being neglected or forgotten, particularly in this area of stable human communities. How did a species whose success was based on social skills come apart at exactly the moment we were finally connected? Has something that worked before been abandoned now?

The answer must be yes, which is painful when you consider just how good we've been at making and maintaining communities of friends throughout our long shared history. Name any second in the history of *Homo sapiens* and you have direct ancestors there, successfully raising children who in turn survive to raise children of their own. That requires a social network. It takes a village. I hope the Villagers will again realize that.

"Survival," in the modern romantic narrative, is painted as some lone act—man against the world. Rugged individuals make for better movies than ordinary folks facing common struggles together. But our human story is not one of loners but of groups, collectives, communities, friends. Knowing you can rely on someone, and they can rely on you, is one of the most fulfilling of human interactions. There is profound mutual benefit there, yes, but also profound joy. The spark of human connection is second only to the spark of conception as the human acts that are indistinguishable from magic. I like you, and you like me, and together we won't have to climb these mountains alone.

But everything has changed in the Internet era. It's the "before and after" moment in the story of humanity. It's the connector and disconnector. And I fear that for every second that passes between when I write these sentences and when they're read, the quainter these concerns will sound. Each time something new moves online and stops happening face-to-face, we deplete the world's supply of social capital. That's the scientific term for the value we derive from positive connections between people, and it may be the most important asset in the ecosystem.

On a fundamental level, the more things become automated, the less we will understand one another as individuals, because we will spend less time actually talking to one another. Already, we do our shopping online and go to the cinema on our couch and order food on an app. Hell, we even shop for romantic partners online, eliminating the need to actually go out and talk to many different people in search of a spark.

For years now, the one thing that forced adult interaction—employment—has been going through a seismic shift so great that it has been called the fourth industrial revolution: steam, electrical, digital . . . telecommuting? The number of people who work from home is growing and growing with no end in sight, and the arrival of the coronavirus only accelerated it. But already, it had spawned a counter industry of "co-working" spaces where people pay good money to share office space because they've realized that working in isolation is not all blissful solitude.

It all fits in with our myth of "busy," which is celebrated in our culture, held up as some kind of badge of success. There are two major problems with this. First, as a matter of fact, we're less busy now than ever, and automation has no doubt helped with that. Those hours you waste dumb-thumbing through Instagram or trying to choose something to watch on Netflix don't count as busy. And second, one must not confuse a "busy life" with a "full life." That bait and switch has gone on too long. So I'll repeat again: We've been misinformed by the misinformed.

But most concerning to me, especially as a parent, is how

much of life is now filled up by social media. I wasted too much of my life scrolling through Facebook and Instagram, and there's zero chance I'm going back on the sauce. Fundamentally, I feel more positive about people. I really do. I also think of them more as actual people, rather than as personas. That's because my interactions happen in person, or using a private person-to-person technology, such as a phone call or email or text message. Without fail, those interactions feel much more likely to end with a positive deposit to the bank of social capital.

This is the world the Villagers will grow up in, and I cannot hide my children from it. They will come of age in a world of increasingly specific villages, hastened by the Internet, where there are subthreads within subforums within subcultures, each of which exists to emphasize a difference rather than highlight a broader similarity. And so my moniker, the Villagers, is a challenge for them to think generationally, not as "us" and "them" but as "we"—to recognize that their villages (for they will belong to many) must align to form our society. That is the long story of the evolution of human culture, and it cannot be abandoned. Instead, it must be challenged to move forward.

And as a father, my own challenge will be the same as it has been for generations of fathers before me, which is to teach my sons "how to be a man" in the world they were born into. It's a task that must balance the intrinsic truths of the genetic code inside the male *Homo sapiens* but shed the learned bad habits of what men are "supposed to be." In a wonderful essay for *Salon*, the sociologist Lisa Wade wrote that "to be close friends, men need to be willing to confess their insecurities, to be kind to others, have empathy and sometimes sacrifice their own self-interest. 'Real Men,' though, are not supposed to do these things. They are supposed to be self-interested, competitive, non-emotional, strong (with no insecurities at all), and able to deal with their emotional problems without help. Being a good friend, then, as well as needing a good friend, is the equivalent of being girly."

Those prescriptions have brought us to where we are: a generation of men who suck at friendship. But one of the great things about parental generations is they all share the desire for their children to avoid the mistakes they made. I'm from Generation X, who perfected an air of detachment and whatever. Now we're obsessed with keeping our kids socially and emotionally engaged in ways that would have felt foreign to us. The slackers of yesterday are the helicopter parents of today.

My children's school has a Buddy Bench in the playground, where a kid can sit if they're feeling excluded. Had that been around when I was a schoolyard kid, no one would have gone near it for fear of being ridiculed. It would have been ten times worse than sitting alone in the cafeteria. I once asked my older son if he would ever feel hesitant to use the bench, and he honestly did not understand the question. Why would he feel awkward to admit he was feeling left out and needed a friend?

These were the things racing through my head as I was finishing this book. And the naïve dreamer in me wished I could build some sort of Buddy Bench for the world, to force them to see that it's okay to say you just needed a friend to sit with.

Then the coronavirus arrived.

• • •

When the world was quickly forced into isolation, we began perhaps the most acute stretch of loneliness in human history. The entire world went through it together, acutely aware of it, and willing to talk about it because that's really all there was to talk about. Instead of the philosophical question of *"Why* aren't we hanging out?" we were all faced with the concrete question of *"When* can we hang out?"

Social science tells us that we form our strongest bonds when we're going through something together, for it presents us with the opportunities to experience the magic of feeling necessary to one another. Such opportunities are in short supply in modern adulthood. Rarely must we demonstrate a commitment to the common good. Yet the desire to make such a contribution is inside us. It's hardwired. It's why "pro-social acts," as they're known, are rewarded with the release of feel-good hormones inside the body.

But even in the modern world, there's a proven way to get there en masse. An opportunity that, when it presents itself, unleashes that desire like nothing else, yielding the strongest societal glue we have. And I hoped like hell that I'd never see it happen.

Mass calamities are awful in every way. Every way except one, for they force us to return home, to the tribal animals we spent millions of years evolving into. When the shit truly hits the fan, we're provided with the chance to fulfill the basic definition of community, of tribe, which is to have one another's back.

Yet where the standard calamity playbook called for people to come together, this crisis demanded that we stay apart. At least physically. As much of the world went into lockdown, two health crises arrived simultaneously: the virus, and the loneliness born of the isolation it forced upon everyone as we fought to stop its spread. Never before in the history of mankind have so many been so alone.

But from that dark void, an unmistakable trend emerged. People immediately began to rally around their tribal connections. Suddenly, I found myself in a group text chain with every squad I'd ever been a member of. High school friends. College buddies. My crew from journalism school. My brother and cousins. My friends from the gym. A crew I'd played bar trivia with a decade before. The guys from my *Survivor* fantasy league.

My phone vibrated roughly every eight seconds, mostly with the latest iteration of a meme involving a naked man with a gargantuan penis, but it served the simple function of keeping in touch. Just in case.

Then there were the group video chats. Those technologies had been sitting around for years, unloved, the bane of the remote worker forced to suffer through virtual meetings. Then overnight they became the virtual campfire, a place to unwind together at the ends of those uncertain days.

Heck, I even started making actual phone calls, and I hate the phone.

None of these things, interestingly, would be categorized as "social media." Instead, everyone turned to the connection platforms that are best described as "tribal media." Organically and instinctively, the squads were assembling.

"What catastrophes seem to do—sometimes in the span of a few minutes—is turn back the clock on ten thousand years of social evolution," Sebastian Junger wrote in his wonderful book *Tribe*. "There is no survival outside group survival, and that creates a social bond that people sorely miss."

I've come to subscribe to the increasingly popular belief that much of our modern angst, anxiety, and disconnect can be traced to our abandonment of the tribal living we were built for. And in the strangest way—digitally, in physical isolation—we were demonstrating, more clearly than ever, the desire for a return.

As the lockdown gradually lifted and life inched back toward some sense of normalcy, we held our first new Wednesday Night. This time, I didn't try to gather the whole group. I limited it to my three newest best friends.

A best friend isn't a person. It's a tier. Mindy Kaling said this once on a television show, and it electrified me the moment I heard it, for I felt immediately freed me from some strange rule of best-friendship I'd been following.

I've had many best friends through the years, beginning with my cousin and my brother. Then came various classmates and teammates, but always I viewed "best friend" as a title only one or two people could hold at once or else it would lose its value. For the longest time, I awarded that title to Mark and Rory, my buddies from high school, a shared milestone that seemed to be the cutoff point for best-friend formation.

But it's much better to think of best friend–ship as a tier, a podium that many can ascend rather than a pedestal belonging to one or two. Embracing this notion has allowed me to enjoy my new relationships without feeling like I'm betraying my old ones. Mark and Rory are still my best friends. So are my brother and my cousin. So are all the ones who came in between. So are all the ones who came after.

During the lockdown, I was happy to discover—or perhaps to allow myself to admit—that I had three new best friends: Kevin, Jon, and Andrew. I was in contact with each of them nearly every day, even as the larger Wednesday Night group went on a COVID-19 hold.

They were the three guys I was most actively friends with when I started the experiment, but back then I doubt that any of us would have referred to the other as a best friend, even if I was spending more time hanging out with them than I was with the people who held that title. Yet when the pandemic hit and we found ourselves circling the wagons, I had more contact with them than any previous titleholders. And when the weather warmed and the restrictions slowly lifted and it was clear we could have our first socially distant outdoor get-together, none of us suggested rallying the whole crew again. Instead, we made plans among ourselves. Kevin had been kind enough to buy us a boat in the off-season, so we made that our thing.

I'm not sure what will become of the Odd Wednesdays. I still love all those guys, and I sincerely hope we'll be able to pull off a gathering here and there for all eternity. But if I'm honest, the fraternity never actually took off. It was kind of a dud.

My grand idea had been a failure.

All I was left with were three best friends to hang out with on Wednesday nights.

What a loser I am.

Lorne Michaels, the creator of *Saturday Night Live*, likes to say that his show doesn't go on because it's ready. It goes on because it's 11:30. And it's in this vein that I find myself trying to wrap up this journey, at least in the pages of this book, because the fine folks at Simon & Schuster made me sign a contract promising that I would. The problem is that I'm still in the middle of my friendship story, and I will remain here until a head count is taken at my funeral.

The person I was at the start of this journey is fundamentally different from the person I am now. It makes me cringe when I hear other people say this, but I'm in a really good place. My friends are a priority in my life, and I believe they will remain that way forever. Even better is that I feel like a priority in their lives as well. When I raised my hand and admitted to being a bit of a loser, I gave myself, and so many of my friends, just the right amount of lubricant to loosen up relationships that were stuck in place. It's happened in all the big important ways, but also in countless small ones. One weekend, my buddy Will drove up from Providence, Rhode Island, and my buddy Scott drove down from Portland, Maine, and we spent the weekend reviving our *Survivor* fantasy league. Another weekend, I went with Rory and our buddies

Patrick and Joe to Lowell, Massachusetts, to revisit the grave of Jack Kerouac, something the four of us had done when we were teenage literary wannabes.

I had also reestablished contact with a guy named Timmy, one of my childhood buddies from Southie—one of these classic Boston guys with the accent and the attitude—and that relationship meant so much more after Timmy was hit by a car and suffered a traumatic brain injury. And I made a new best friend on the train, of all places, a guy named Jody who has been trying and failing to turn me into a bow hunter and spearfisherman. I have yet to actually shoot anything, but I look fantastic in camouflage.

The list goes on and on, and I'm committed to making sure it will go on and on.

When I set off on this quest I had registered my score on the UCLA Loneliness Scale, and my plan all along had been retake the test when 11:30 arrived. But I'm not getting back on the scale.

My relationships are better. And better is always better. That's enough for me.

The text message arrived just before 2:00 a.m., but I didn't see it until the following morning. I immediately started panicking.

It had been a few weeks since I'd last talked to Rory, and I was under the impression that he was doing great. He had been dating a new girl for more than a year, and they seemed like an easy fit. She was nice, and fun to hang out with, and at one point he had forced a laughing sigh out of me when he said, "I didn't know relationships could be this easy."

But shit . . . as I read his text over again, I had to admit I really didn't know the last time I'd spoken to him. Maybe a few weeks was actually a month. Maybe more. Had we really fallen into this trap again? I was worried.

"Hey, man," he had written. "It's late and you will obviously think 'Oh Rory,' but the truth is . . . I really miss you. Can we hang without a plan or activity? I could really be into a best friend right now . . . or tomorrow, or whenever you can."

I wrote back as soon as I got the message. "Dude, call me when you get up!"

I gave it an hour and then I called him. Then I called him again. Then I called him a third time. Then I seriously considered calling in the cavalry.

Finally, about eight hours after his original text, he finally responded to me.

"In meetings till 2. Will call after."

Fucking Rory.

When we finally got on the phone, he told me he was just down in the dumps because of his legal battle with Cersei, which had been dragging on for more than a year as they tried to divvy up the house and the business and everything else they owned together. Lawyers were draining his bank account; the fighting was sucking the life out of him; and he just wanted it to be over so he could finally move on.

I was glad it was not something worse, of course. But I must confess that I was mad at him for making me think it was. When I told my wife this and showed her the text, she shook her head and gave me that look. I had it all wrong, she said.

205

"That's a huge accomplishment for both of you. That never would have happened before. He never would have tried to reach out to you in the middle of the night if he was feeling sad."

She walked away, and I read the text again, with new eyes, as she called back to me from the other room.

"I feel like that's the end of your book right there."

Acknowledgments

Writing a book is not a solitary act. It requires friends, and I've been fortunate to have had some great ones on my side from the beginning. At the *Boston Globe*, Francis Storrs set me off on this quest, and Brian McGrory, Jen Peter, Steve Wilmsen, and Nestor Ramos have been incredible allies in helping this project reach the end. Richard Abate at 3Arts worked his magic to connect me with the perfect editor for this story, Jofie Ferrari-Adler at Simon & Schuster, who, along with Carolyn Kelly, made this a collaborative project that was more rewarding than I could ever have imagined.

I was born lucky in that I have two great parents, Billy and Rachel, who instilled a love of storytelling in me from the beginning, and a grandmother, Rosalia, who has always showered me with encouragement.

Then there are my best friends, those people who have made this long, strange journey we call life into a roller coaster of fun: Jack, Tommy, Michael, Jamie, Timmy, Rory, Mark, Michelle, Kristin, Mike, John, Steve, Brittney, Catherine, Kathy, Kathleen, Sara, Joe, Patrick, Nick, Dan, Matt, Rob, Farrell, Rhaoul, Scott, Chuck,

Melissa, Amy, Iqbal, Darren, Victor, Emily, Angie, April, Carter, Arrin, Andrew, Jim, Tim, Tom, Sheila, Jon, Kevin, Jill, Chris, Kara, Whitney, Jaime, Dianne, Brian, George, Johnny, Odessa, Jordan, Sridevi, Zac, Kyle, Pat, Giselle, Ryan, Lindsey, Gerry, Erik, Jay, Jason, Stubba, Will, Akilah, Tracy, Martine, Dina, Maria, Beth, Jessica, Aram, Andrew, Jen, Josh, Eric, Sam, Amber, Rebecca, Jody, Chad, Heather, Robin, Brooke, Casey, Eliran, Jonti, Theresa, Ashley, and even Nathan. It's been too long, y'all; we need to hang out.

And most important, my lovely wife, Lori, and our sweet boys, Charlie and Jake, make each day better than the last. You're more than just family. You're my friends.

About the Author

BILLY BAKER is a staff writer for the *Boston Globe*. He lives on Cape Ann with his wife, Lori, and their sons, Charlie and Jake.